3.85

GAINING POWER

DEMOCRACY AND ELECTIONS IN CANADA

LONGMAN CANADA LIMITED

JOHN A. MILLER / DONALD A. HURST

Gaining Power

Democracy and Elections in Canada

Acknowledgements

The authors and publisher wish to thank the following for permission to reproduce copyright material. Every effort has been made to acknowledge copyright. Any errors or ommissions drawn to our attention will be corrected in future editions.

From "Dad in jail because son's not in school" reprinted by permission of *The Spectator*. From *You'll never die, John A.* by Edwin C. Guillet, reprinted by permission of the Macmillan Company of Canada Limited. From *Poking into politics* by Grant MacEwan, reprinted by permission of Western Producer Prairie Books. From an article by W.A. Wilson in *The Montreal Star*, October 25, 1973, reprinted by permission of Canada Wide Feature Service Limited. From *Louis St. Laurent—Canadian* by Dale Thomson, reprinted by permission of The Macmillan Company of Canada Limited. From *The Chief* by Thomas Van Dusen, reprinted by permission of the author. From *Assignment Ottawa* by Peter Dempson, reprinted by permission of General Publishing Co., Ltd. From *Pendulum of Power* by J.M. Beck, reprinted by permission of Prentice-Hall of Canada, Ltd. Norris cartoon reprinted by permission of *The Vancouver Sun*. Macpherson cartoon reprinted with permission *Toronto Star*. From "Is charisma the key to solving the Trudeau mystery" by Anthony Westell, reprinted by permission of *The Globe and Mail*. From "Stanfield, an image of trivia and cliché" by Martin O'Malley, reprinted by permission of *The Globe and Mail*. "Redesigning Robert": Christopher Beacom quotation reprinted by permission of *Maclean's*. From "For the sake of argument" by J. Scott, reprinted by permission of the author. From "Politics: where the money comes from", reprinted by permission of CFPL Broadcasting Limited. From *Divide and con* by Walter Stewart, reprinted by permission of New Press, Don Mills, Ontario. From "Peter Maloney lost an election" by Hartley Steward, reprinted by permission of the author. "PC Candidate's Calendar" reproduced by permission of the Progressive Conservative Party of Canada. This or any other Party material may not be reproduced in any way without the permission of the Progressive Conservative Party of Canada. From "Leadership central issue in battle" by Peter Meerburg, reprinted by permission of the author and *The Halifax Chronicle-Herald*. "Second canvass reminder" reprinted by permission of the New Democratic Party of Ontario. From *Journey to power* by Donald Peacock, reprinted by permission of McGraw-Hill Ryerson Limited. Royal memorandum on the choice of Ottawa as capital of Canada reproduced with the gracious permission of Her Majesty The Queen. "The Prime Minister's Residence": quotations from *Hansard* reproduced by permission of Information Canada. "And what did you think of Ottawa": quotation from Jacques Greber, *Master Plan for the National Capital,* reproduced by permission of Information Canada. From "It's not easy running the littlest embassy in Ottawa" by Tom Alderman, reprinted by permission of *The Canadian Magazine*. Facsimile of the petition to the Queen from the Province of Canada, March 16 , 1857, reproduced by permission of the Public Record Office, London.

The authors and publisher would also like to thank the following for their contributions of original material to the book: Mr. Rob Welch, Mr. Andrew Tin, Mayor Arthur Phillips, Premier Alexander B. Campbell, The Rt. Hon. John Diefenbaker, and Flora MacDonald, MP.

Photo Credits

Boris Spremo: 18 Canadian Press: 5, 36, 61, 76, 78 The Whig-Standard: 7 The Spectator: 11 Archives of Ontario: 27, 29, 31, 91, 93 Miller Services: 33, 79, 98 The Toronto Sun: 34, 60, 67 Liberal Party of Canada: 39 ©Karsh, Ottawa: 45 Ernst Zundel (retouching of Stanfield photos): 46, 47 Lynn Ball: 73 Ontario Ministry of Industry and Tourism: 88, 89, 94, 96, 99 Public Archives of Canada: 92

To V.F. Fullerton

Contents

Unit 1

An introduction to Canadian democracy

A student leader speaks out

Rob Welch has served as the Prime Minister of the Student Parliament at Sir Winston Churchill Secondary School in St. Catharines, Ontario. Rob's father is an Ontario provincial government Cabinet Minister.

It's funny. For as long as I can remember, government has interested me. So when opportunities to get into an aspect of politics come, I usually take them, because if you put enough effort into these things, you are bound to get more out of them.

I say this because I feel the most important part of public affairs is being with people and understanding their views. One does not have to agree with these views, but by making a good effort to find out about individuals' ideas, part of the problem of conflict people face is solved.

I am closing out a year as Prime Minister of a school student parliament, a student government based on the parliamentary system. In Cabinet, conflicts of ideas come up all the time. Nothing will happen if a government cannot make up its mind, so what I have tried to do is explore each member's ideas, understand their views, and take the best points of them in order to build a piece of legislation.

Besides the interaction in Cabinet, you have to listen to the Student Parliament, finding out why members support or reject legislation, and ultimately you have to communicate with the students, giving your views on policy and listening to those of the people you are acting for.

Synonymous with contact with students comes contact with Administration and Staff members. You have to be firm with your views, but it is your responsibility to respect these people's views.

So I back up my feelings about understanding and communication being most important in public affairs by telling what I have to do as a head of a student government. But another point was made about the relationship between the effort you make and the rewards you get from being involved. I think this ties in with what was said with regard to understanding people's ideas. For if you have learned how to do this, your life will be a lot easier for you in dealings with other people.

If you can listen, talk and compromise, you can avoid conflict. This is the thing about democracy that is important, the regard one has for the other person's view. Myself, I would much rather have conflicting ideas heard and explored and an eventual solution effected, than have conflict without an interchange of ideas where the only solution is a separation of sorts.

This is what you get out of your efforts, an invaluable experience in accepting other people. It is a skill you will use again and again. It helps you do things for people, which is really not such a bad thing either.

1/Getting involved

Beyond the world of student governments lie plenty more opportunities to get involved in public affairs. For many citizens it seems that high school, however, is an ideal place to get started.

Consider the following five cases.

Andrew Tin, Student Campaign Worker, Stoney Creek, Ontario

I only officially joined the Young New Democrats this year, but I have been involved with the party for about two years. As a member of the NDP, I am entitled to vote on party affairs and go to party happenings. During elections, I work to try and elect my candidate by delivering leaflets, scrutineering, and doing odd jobs around the campaign headquarters. I do these things because I believe in the aims of the NDP and hope to see them fulfilled during my lifetime.

Arthur Phillips, Mayor of Vancouver

I must confess that I did not have much interest in politics in high school. I was much more interested in sports and girls.

My interests broadened out somewhat in university days to include economics and a number of other academic subjects. However, it was not until I was about 30 years old that I really became interested in politics. At that time, John Diefenbaker was the Prime Minister and I thought he was making a mess of running the country. As a result, I got interested in working for a very outstanding Liberal candidate in the riding in which I live and helped him get elected.

My interest dwindled off somewhat for a few years in the middle 60's but became active again in 1968. At that time the focus was on civic affairs, which I thought were being very badly handled by the civic administration in Vancouver. A number of us got together and formed a new civic political organization, called TEAM, which fielded candidates in the 1968 civic elections. I was one of those who were elected Aldermen at that time and subsequently went on to run for Mayor four years later.

5

Alexander B. Campbell, Premier of Prince Edward Island

I became personally involved in politics as a young boy, my father having taken an active part in the governing of the Province of Prince Edward Island. I took an active part in the Liberal Party organization over the years and was eventually asked in the spring of 1965 to run in a by-election in my constituency of 5th Prince. Later, following my election, on December 11, 1965, I was elected Leader of the Liberal Party of Prince Edward Island, and within sixteen months of the by-election, I was sworn in as Premier of Prince Edward Island following the General Election in the spring of 1966.

The Rt. Hon. John G. Diefenbaker, Thirteenth Prime Minister of Canada

During my early high school days I tried over and over again to make speeches, but with little success. Later on I belonged to the first Boys' Parliament in Canada, which met in Regina in 1911. I made several speeches there.

It was in the University of Saskatchewan that I learned the rules of Parliament, and that has been helpful to me through the years. There I belonged to a University Parliament which met regularly and dealt with matters that had recently been before the House of Commons. A professor who understood the rules presided as Speaker, and the knowledge gained from him is something for which I have always been grateful.

From my earliest days, beginning in public school, I determined the course of action to which I would devote my life. My parents moved from East Toronto to the Fort Carlton area in August, 1903. Immigration from Continental Europe was under way. I felt that these immigrants, along with the Indians and Métis, were being discriminated against because of their race. I determined to spend my life bringing about an end to discrimination based on race and colour. It took a long time under law; indeed it took me half a century of advocacy of a Bill of Rights before its enactment in 1960.

Flora MacDonald, MP, Kingston and The Islands

The world of politics is exciting, demanding, frustrating and stimulating. To appreciate it fully you have to be part of it. The astute observer, no matter how penetrating his analysis, can have at best a limited appreciation of the wide range of activities of the involved politician.

How did I become involved? There was no conscious decision taken to become a politician. Like others of my generation I thought of traditional careers — nurse, secretary, teacher — the options were limited. And yet the seeds of interest were sown when, as a youngster, I trotted along with my father to all kinds of political meetings. In those pre-TV days my dad thought it was important to make his own personal assessment of any political leader who visited our remote part of the country, and he would spare no effort to attend any political gathering — Liberal, Tory or Socialist. For company he would often take me along.

He, himself, as a child had heard Sir John A. Macdonald and Sir Charles Tupper, and his interest in politics, unabated over the years, was passed along to me.

Later, in my late teens and early twenties, when I travelled and worked in all parts of Canada and the United Kingdom, I found it fascinating to visit Parliaments and Legislatures to listen to debates and watch the finesse of politics as played on the floor of the Chamber. In Britain I listened to Winston Churchill and Clement Atlee, in Toronto to Leslie Frost and, in Ottawa, to John Diefenbaker.

And so it was that this long-time interest flourished. It focussed first on personalities, then on issues and, eventually, became the dominant interest in my own life.

Flora MacDonald meets the voters.

QUESTION

1. What patterns of getting involved do you see in these five case studies?

2/The long arm of the law

Life can bring lots of bewildering experiences. Some young people must make decisions about friends or religion or courses in school that will affect them all their lives. Sometimes it is a tougher task to take stock of what you stand for or to develop your personality so that you're happy with yourself. Other young people feel life is an endless struggle with parents.

At home your parents have probably established a set of rules which they expect you to follow. You may not always agree with their rules.

If you make up your mind to stay out on Wednesday night until midnight and your parents say you must be in before ten o'clock, you are about to challenge a rule made by your parents.

Communities, too, have rules. You can probably guess the consequences if you should try to park a car in the middle of the road or try to make your living by stealing other people's property.

There are community rules called laws which tell you where you can park. There are laws which protect other people's property and stop you from taking it for yourself. And these same laws tell what punishment you may receive if you refuse to respect them.

Meeting these laws and trying to live with them can be another bewildering experience for young people. This is especially true if you find it difficult to understand why a law was made or if you disagree with its details.

This book is about laws in Canada — who makes them, how they are made, how they affect you, what you can do about them.

Far back in the history of man our ancestors decided that they did not want to live without rules. They did not want to live in a state of anarchy. They wanted a set of rules which affected everybody in their communities.

Making laws

QUESTIONS

1. Make a list of community rules or laws which puzzle or anger you.
2. Why do you think people felt it was necessary to have laws in their communities?

The decision of our ancestors to have laws has obviously affected you and Canada. Consider these three examples.

Who controls the music you hear?

Turn on your radio. Listen to the disc jockey who is saying, "... That was record number twelve on the Top Sixty. Pick up your free copy of the Top Sixty Survey at your neighbourhood record bar today. And now, to take us up to newstime, the chart-buster everybody's calling to request. Here's ..."

The number and the kind of records any Canadian radio station can play are carefully controlled by our national government. The Canadian Radio and Television Commission is an agency of the government in Ottawa which was set up to regulate broadcasting throughout the country.

In 1970 this Commission announced the following rule:

> At least 30% of the musical compositions broadcast by a station or network operator between the hours of 6:00 a.m. and 12 midnight shall be by a Canadian and shall be scheduled in a reasonable manner throughout such period.

The Commission then specified that after January 18, 1972, a piece of music could be considered Canadian only if it met two of the following conditions:

> (a) the instrumentation or lyrics were principally performed by a Canadian,
> (b) the music was composed by a Canadian,
> (c) the lyrics were written by a Canadian,
> (d) the live performance was wholly recorded in Canada.

The CRTC has another rule that all stations keep a log or daily list of their songs and commercials to be checked at any time by a government inspector.

1. Suppose you were the disc jockey with the job to select the records for the next hour. Make a log of the 15 songs that you would submit to be played on your show.
2. Beside the songs on your list indicate how you are complying with the CRTC regulations for the national government.
3. Why would our national government make such regulations?

Who makes rules about your schooling?

The following article from the Hamilton *Spectator* illustrates how another type of government rule affects some citizens.

DAD IN JAIL BECAUSE SON'S NOT IN SCHOOL

A Mountain father is in jail today because he wouldn't send his 15-year-old son to high school.

Dennis Douglas, 44, of Upper James Street, has been in Barton Street Jail since Monday when he refused in family court to post a $100 bond pledging his son John would return to school.

It was his second conviction for violating the Schools Administration Act, which compels parents to ensure all their children under age 16 attend school.

The charges against Mr. Douglas were laid by Hamilton board of education officials after repeated warnings and consultations with him and his wife.

Although John's 16th birthday is not until October, he is only obligated to attend school until June when the current school term ends.

"My husband has gone to jail on a point of principle," said Marjorie Douglas, John's mother, in an interview yesterday.

"We have no intention of sending John back to school until he shows he wants to go. John was failing Grade 9 for the second time and was getting absolutely nothing out of school."

At his father's suggestion, John withdrew from classes at Westmount Secondary School last December, two months after his 15th birthday.

Mr. Douglas put John to work assisting in the family fish and chip store at Upper James Street and Limeridge Road.

Signs in the window of the store warned

customers yesterday the business would be closed because the proprietor is in jail.

One sign reads: "Robbed son of six months babysitting privileges (school). GUILTY. Ten days jail!"

Says another: "Temporary residence: Barton Street Jail."

In Mr. Douglas's first family court appearance, he paid a $25.00 fine rather than go to jail.

To a second charge this week, Mr. Douglas was offered a choice by Judge David Steinberg of signing a $100 bond or serving 10 days in jail. He chose jail.

"It's just a form of blackmail you pay the court to keep your child out of school," said Mrs. Douglas.

As far as we're concerned, the whole educational system has gone to pot. They're not one bit concerned about the individual. They're only concerned about the letter of the law and the regulations."

Mrs. Douglas, who lives in a well-furnished brick home across the street from the school, said the family could well afford the $100 fine but refused to pay on principle.

Prior to this year, the Douglas's paid more than $1,000 a year to send John, the eldest of three children, to the private Hillcrest College.

"He had just scraped through school right along and hadn't done a stitch of work. It was just a waste of his time and everybody else's."

The man in this story was disputing a rule made by another government. This time it was not the national government but the provincial government of Ontario.

In Ontario the following law tells who must attend school and when:

Every child who attains the age of six years after the first school day in September in any year shall attend an elementary or secondary school on every school day from the first school day in September in the next succeeding year until the last school day in June in the year in which he attains the age of sixteen years.

QUESTIONS

1. Do you agree with the stand taken by Mr. Douglas in keeping his son out of school even though this broke the provincial law? Why?
2. What changes in the law would you suggest if you had the power to decide when students could leave school in Ontario?
3. Investigate how the Department of Education in your own province regulates school attendance.
4. What other rules from your province's Department of Education affect you as a student?

Who is responsible for fireworks rules?

One Canadian community passed this law concerning the sale and use of fireworks. It is an example of the rules of a third type of government whose ideas affect young people.

No person shall display, offer for sale, or sell fireworks, squibs, fireballs or firecrackers within the limits of the City excepting on the day being observed as Victoria Day and for three days prior to the day being observed as Victoria Day; provided that if such three day period include a Sunday, the Sunday shall not be counted as one of the three days.

No person shall sell any fireworks, squibs, fireballs or firecrackers to any person under the age of 18 years.

No person shall discharge any fireworks, squibs, fireballs or firecrackers within the limits of the City at any time during the whole of the year excepting on the day being observed as Victoria Day.

Notwithstanding the provisions of this by-law, a group or organization may, with the approval of City Council, hold a fireworks display on any day in the year, excepting Sundays, and for such purposes may purchase and persons may sell fireworks for such display.

QUESTIONS

1. This rule is called a by-law from a local government. What do you feel prompted such a by-law?
2. What other local by-laws affect young people in your area?
3. Which local by-laws would particularly interest your parents?

How do governments divide up the areas they control?

Canada has three types of government — national, provincial and local. Anyone journeying leisurely from Newfoundland to British Columbia would meet a variety of laws from a number of governments across the country. But every law the traveller would meet comes from one of the three types of governments.

Some of the laws would apply to every part of the nation. These would be laws made by our national government. Because our national government takes care of postal services, for example, it sets the mail rates for the country. No matter where the tourist stops in Canada, the cost of sending a post card home will always be the same.

Canada has one national government. It meets in Ottawa and its members come from every part of the country. Our national government might be described as the senior level of government.

On his trip the tourist would also be affected by the laws of each of the provinces he visits. Canada has ten provincial governments. Each one is composed of representatives from all sections of that province. Provincial government could be described as the intermediate level of government.

Laws regulating highway traffic are examples of the responsibilities of the provincial governments. The maximum speed limit on a road which passes between provinces can change at a provincial boundary. Because each provincial government is free to control the flow of traffic on roads within its own territory, different speed limits may be in force along the road.

The third level of government is the local or municipal government. This is the junior level, even though municipal governments greatly outnumber the national and provincial governments.

If our tourist decides to go shopping in the communities he visits, he might find the variety of hours for store businesses equal to the number of communities where he stops. This is because each municipal government has the power to regulate the times when the stores in its area are open.

QUESTION

1. Each level of government must collect money to pay for the services it offers its citizens. Find out the kinds of taxes which you and your parents pay to your federal, provincial and municipal governments.

Why do we have three levels of government?

The decision to have three levels of government in Canada was actually made over a century ago. The Fathers of Confederation had the task of organizing the new Canada before 1867, and it was they who drew up the guidelines to tell just how the young nation would operate.

Among the delegates at the Charlottetown and Quebec Conferences there came a recognition that, while the different areas wanted to be part of the new country, each one had certain characteristics that it wanted to retain. Each area felt it should keep some power to look after its own, unique business.

Men like Leonard Tilley from New Brunswick and Charles Tupper from Nova Scotia argued that only Maritimers could understand what type of laws the Atlantic colonies needed just for their own region.

George Cartier who lived in Canada East described the feelings of Canadians descended from the original French settlers. His people spoke a different language; their cultural background was unique; their religious beliefs were different from those of many of the other people in British North America.

Everyone finally agreed that there should be a national government to take care of items which affected all parts of the country. A separate level of government would be organized to look after regional affairs, just as Tilley, Tupper and Cartier had suggested. Local business, as usual, could be handled by the municipal government.

The system of organizing a nation with a strong national government and weaker regional governments is called a federal system of government. Canadians often use the term federal when they refer to the government in Ottawa.

In 1864 at the Quebec Conference, John A. Macdonald put forward this motion:

That the best interest and present and future prosperity of British North America will be promoted by a Federal Union under the Crown of Great Britain, provided such union can be effected on principles just to the several provinces.

Macdonald's motion was eventually accepted by the delegates at the conference. Then they moved on to the difficult job of deciding what specific tasks or powers would be given to the various levels of government.

The decisions they made were suggested to the British government in London. Because the colonies in British North America were like Britain's children, the Canadians had to ask for permission if they wanted to undertake major changes in their affairs.

On March 29, 1867, the British Parliament passed The British North America Act to create Canada. The new nation, according to this British law, was to be born officially on July 1, 1867.

The BNA Act set down some of the ways in which Canada was to be organized. Some of its most important sections listed the powers of the federal and provincial levels of government just as the Fathers of Confederation had recommended after their meetings in Quebec.

Although parts of the BNA Act have been changed over the past century, the Act has remained very much the same as it was originally. It is still the basis of how Canada is organized and governed.

Here are some of the responsibilities which the BNA Act assigned to the federal and provincial governments:

Federal Responsibilities
  Regulating trade and commerce
  Raising money by any means of taxation
  Directing the postal service
  National Defence
  Controlling navigation and shipping
  Supervising coastal and inland fisheries

Controlling national currency and coinage
Indians and their lands
Criminal law
Building, maintaining, and managing penitentiaries
Carrying on any necessary activities which are not given to the provincial governments but which are needed for the peace, order, and good government of Canada

Provincial Responsibilities
Education
Supervising municipal governments in the province
Administering provincial justice and laws
Building, maintaining and managing provincial reformatories and prisons
Raising money by direct taxation
Regulating marriages
Controlling the sale and use of alcoholic beverages

QUESTIONS

1. What advantages does a federal system of government have for a nation like Canada?
2. Many nations are organized with a federal system of government. From your library research give the names of two such nations. Beside each country write the term it gives to its intermediate level of government.
3. What problems might develop in a nation with a federal system of government?
4. Although Great Britain is now moving towards a federal system of government, it has had a *unitary* system of government for many years. Find out what is meant by a unitary system of government.
5. If you were organizing a new nation, what conditions might you check before deciding whether to have a unitary or federal system of government?
6. There are two types of taxes: direct taxes and indirect taxes. The BNA Act says that the federal government may levy each kind and the provincial government may levy only direct taxes. Find examples to illustrate each of these types.
7. This is the time to begin charts to illustrate the federal and provincial governments' responsibilities. In one column of each chart list the powers of the governments as decribed above. Watch your newspaper for the name of the government department which carries out each responsibility. Try to find the name and the picture of the Minister who directs each department. When you have the name of the department, the name of its Minister and his picture, add these to the chart.

In addition, watch for other departments and other Ministers who carry out responsibilities not listed above. You may add these to the charts as you find them.

3/Everybody has a point of view

Bobby Clark, Bobby Orr, Bernie Parent ...

By the time you start this sentence your mind has probably told you that these three men have something in common. They are all hockey players.

If the names had been Betsy Clifford and Nancy Greene, you would have thought of skiing. Russ Jackson brings football to mind, just as Ferguson Jenkins's name stands for baseball.

All these people could be classified as athletes, but each one has a special area of athletics in which he or she excels.

As a group, all Canadians can be classified as citizens. This means that they call Canada their home country and take part in the affairs of our nation. But just as the term "athlete" does not tell you the specialty of each person we named earlier, so the word "citizen" does not tell you very much about each Canadian.

It is possible to place Canadians in other, clearer categories to know more about them. You can classify them by the area in which they live, by their sex, their occupation or their religion. In fact, whenever the federal government undertakes a complete survey or census of our population, these are some of the categories it uses.

Another method of classifying people is according to the way they believe laws should be made and national issues settled. This category is based on each citizen's political views.

What are your views? Where do you stand?

Here is a list of statements describing how some interesting matters in Canada may be approached. Each statement expresses a definite point of view.

Read the list carefully and then, on the second reading, use the following method to indicate how you personally feel about these points of view.

Give yourself three points if you agree completely with a statement, two points if you hesitate to agree with a statement, and one point if you disagree entirely with the statement. Then find the total number of points you have.

1. Laws on the non-medical use of drugs should be maintained and strictly enforced.
2. Cadet Corps should be made compulsory in all high schools to give more discipline to young people.
3. Canada should continue to maintain her ties with the British monarchy.
4. Students would appreciate their education more if it were not all paid for.
5. The death penalty should be mandatory as a punishment for murder.
6. Teenagers ought to spend the summer working rather than travelling across the country.
7. The best motto for any citizen is, "I will support my country whether it is right or wrong!"
8. Every student should sing the national anthem.
9. Instead of looking to the government for assistance, poor people should work harder themselves.
10. The police and the courts are too soft with people who break the law.
11. Individual businessmen can do a better job than any government running Canada's industry and transportation needs.
12. Hard work is the best way to make teenagers into solid citizens.

Scoring
Consider those with scores from 1 to 15 points as group A; from 16 to 22 points as group B; from 23 to 36 points as group C.

QUESTIONS

1. Either as a complete class, or in groups, work out the point of view which the members of each group seem to hold in common.
2. How might the size of the groups be different if your parents instead of you were scoring the quiz? Explain why you believe there might be any change in the group sizes.

How can you classify people's opinions?

Three basic categories are used to classify people's points of view on political matters. Within each category, however, there is room for a great range of opinions.

To indicate where a person stands with his opinions, he can be placed on an imaginary horizontal line which represents all points of view.

At the middle of the line is the place where people with moderate opinions find themselves. This position is called the *centre*. From the centre we refer to different points of view according to the directions, either the *right* (right-wing) or the *left* (left-wing). The use of the terms *right* and *left* to describe political attitudes comes to us from the early days of the French Revolution when the radicals, who wanted sweeping changes in government and society, sat on the left side of the Assembly and the conservatives, who wanted to preserve the old system, sat on the right.

This diagram presents the characteristics of these positions.

QUESTIONS

1. Look back carefully at the twelve statements on page 17. Write a paragraph to tell where you feel these points of view fall on the line of political beliefs. Be sure to use examples.
2. Carefully consider four adults or close friends whom you know very well. For each one write a short paragraph to tell where you think he or she might be placed on the line of political beliefs. Again you must tell your reasons for making each judgment.

LEFT

Have plenty of ideas to change the conditions they see around them

Are willing to let the government own large businesses and means of transportation

Believe the government should care for the less fortunate

Like their country but are not bound tightly to its history and traditions

CENTRE

Have moderate opinions

Believe in law and order where necessary

Are willing to change their minds — not bound to a strict approach or doctrine

Believe in searching for ways to settle problems that are acceptable to the greatest number of people

RIGHT

Are concerned with preserving the country's traditions

Ideas slow to change

Very patriotic

Strongly believe in keeping law and order and discipline for the nation

Believe the role of government should be kept at a minimum so that individuals can have the greatest freedom to do as they wish

Believe industry should be controlled privately and not by the government

What are political parties?

Citizens who share the same needs and wants or the same basic points of view about how Canada should be governed meet together in organizations called political parties. They hope that by working together they can gain control of a government and make laws to satisfy the demands of the citizens whom they represent. They believe that their decisions and changes will be best for the people.

If these citizens want to affect matters which the British North America Act says are federal responsibilities, they join a party organized at the federal level. If they want to affect decisions made in their provincial governments, they work in a provincial party. In some of the larger Canadian municipalities, citizens are beginning to form political parties at this level too.

Parties are important in managing the affairs of a country or province. They act like teams which unite citizens so they can work together to conduct the government business.

Since Confederation, Canada has seen many different political parties. In each one of these the members shared a basic opinion on how to deal with Canadian affairs so that their needs and wants could be satisfied.

Just as a citizen can be placed on the line of political beliefs, so each political party can find a spot on this line. The policies which party members adopt for their organization determine where that party will sit on the scale of political beliefs.

Two Canadian parties, the Liberals and the Progressive Conservatives, have their origins in the earliest years of our nationhood. The two other parties which are active in our national affairs today, the New Democratic Party and the Social Credit Party with its Quebec branch, the *Créditistes*, developed earlier in this century.

QUESTIONS

1. Explain the difference between *conservative* and *Conservative*, and *liberal* and *Liberal*.
2. Select one of the parties mentioned in this section and prepare a study of it. Be sure to include the history of your party, its basic points of view, its accomplishments, and the names of its prominent leaders.
3. Draw an eight-inch horizontal line in your notebook to represent the line of political opinions. On the line mark the basic directions of thought.

As you hear the reports of students who have studied other Canadian parties, be prepared to place these parties on the line.

Now indicate where you believe you personally stand on the line and then place several of your friends or relatives on the line. You must be ready to support your decisions here with definite proof for each party and person.
4. Some Canadian political scientists use the terms *pragmatic* and *ideological* to describe Canadian political parties. Pragmatic refers to parties such as the Liberals and Progressive Conservatives which are close to the centre on the scale of political opinions. Ideological refers to parties of the right- or left-wing. Find out what these terms mean. Try to assess whether this is an accurate way of characterizing Canadian parties. You will probably need to review several party platforms and the current events of the years when the platforms were published to make a sound study of this problem.
5. (a) Compose a federal chart showing the parties, leaders and prominent party members for our national government.

(b) By carefully watching and reading your newspaper build up a chart which shows the names of the political parties in our ten provinces and the leaders of these parties. Try to include pictures of these leaders in your chart.

Unit 2

Winning is just the beginning

World history has far more examples of decisions that have been made *for* the people than of decisions made *by* the people.

In Canada the decision about who will lead the country and what policies will be followed is made when millions of citizens secretly mark their ballots and drop them into metal boxes.

How do these voters make their decisions?

Is a voter influenced by mass-media campaigns which sell politicians and their policies like soft drinks or automobiles?

Can Canadian democracy be genuine if the citizens merely vote every few years?

Who pays for the cost of an election campaign?

But the most important question of all concerns your role in an election. Will one person's vote, *your vote*, make a difference?

As you read through and study the sections of this unit, keep this question uppermost in your mind.

4/The vote getters

Since Confederation, Canadian voters have seen many different campaign styles. The following selections describe how our greatest "vote getters" appealed to the country for support.

Sir John A. Macdonald was Canada's first Prime Minister. He dominated Canadian politics from Confederation in 1867 until his death in 1891. The campaign activity which Macdonald most enjoyed was picnicking with the voters.

In August of the same year another picnic was held at Cobourg. A procession of carriages, with two bands, escorted John A. through streets gaily decorated with cedar arches.

Welcoming Sir John were these slogans: 'Canada's Greatest Statesman', 'See the Conquering Hero Comes!', 'A Thousand Welcomes', 'The Young Men of Cobourg Have Confidence in Sir John', 'The Workingman's Friend', 'We Welcome the Conservative Chief'.

The procession continued with enthusiasm along King Street eastward and south to Boulton's Grove.

Speeches occupied most of the afternoon, and in the evening 'a monstrous torchlight procession' half a mile long, headed by the two bands 'and accompanied by a great number of transparencies and a grand display of fireworks,' led the crowd to Cobourg's distinguished Victoria Hall where the leader again spoke.

From *You'll Never Die, John A!* by Edwin C. Guillet

Sir Wilfrid Laurier

Sir Wilfrid Laurier was Canada's first French-Canadian Prime Minister. His term of office, 1896 to 1911, brought Canada into the twentieth century.

In commanding large crowds, nobody surpassed Sir Wilfrid Laurier who came upon the Canadian scene a short time after Howe, McGee and Davin and was the most finished speaker of his political generation. Years after his passing, students continued to find literary delight in reading the classical utterances of this man who filled his followers with pride and his opponents with disarray.

When he opened his federal election campaign at Sorel, Quebec, on September 28, 1904, it was with an outdoor audience numbering 5,000, and a few days later, he saw another 5,000 people trying to gain entrance to a City of Quebec hall capable of accommodating 1,500. When opening his next election campaign, four years later, and again, at Sorel, 10,000 people were present for the outdoor meeting and heard him proclaim, majestically: "Not many years now remain to me. The snows of winter have taken the place of spring; but ... I feel that I have as much strength as ever for the service of my country." After two hours of speaking, nobody said he talked too long. And an outdoor audience at Niagara Falls, during the same campaign, totalled 20,000.

From *Poking Into Politics* by Grant MacEwan

Y.M.C.A. BUILDING.
BATHS - BOWLING - SWIMMING - POOL
GYMNASIUM - LIBRARY AND READING ROOM
JOIN - TO DAY $5 A YEAR

SIR WILFRED LISTENS
TO THE MUSIC RENDERED BY
THE COBALT BRASS BAND
IN FRONT OF Y.M.C.A.

PHOTO BY McCREA STUDIO

William Lyon Mackenzie King

Mackenzie King holds a world record for being a Prime Minister longer than any other leader. He guided Canada during such crises as the Depression of the 1930's and World War II in the 1940's.

In this selection a noted columnist recalls meeting Mr. King during an election campaign.

My own first contact with Mackenzie King was during the 1935 election when, as a very junior reporter, I had been despatched by a short-staffed editor to the Moncton railway station to interview him during the 20 or 30-minute stop the Ocean Limited made there.

It was Mr. King, rather more than my own inexperience, that made it an unsuccessful interview. He had me into his compartment and before I had even asked a question began quizzing me, asking about each of the city's leading Liberals by name, wanting to know what they were doing in the campaign and, above all, whether they seemed to be working hard.

Near the end of the train's stop he volunteered a few comments about the campaign which I later on constructed into some sort of story. Little as I knew about politics, I was nonetheless surprised that a party leader could be so specific in his questions, naming each person about whose activities he wanted information.

It was not until much later on that I realized that Mr. King could have done the same thing in most of the ridings of Canada and that it was because he had devoted so much time to its organization, and could do that sort of thing, that it had become such a formidable political organization. Any other party leader whom I have watched since then would have needed the briefing of local aides to have performed as Mr. King did during that long-ago conversation in a railway compartment.

From an article by W. A. Wilson in *The Montreal Star*, October 25, 1973

Louis St. Laurent

Louis St. Laurent succeeded Mackenzie King as Prime Minister of Canada in 1951. Canadians, who pictured him as a kind, gentlemanly leader, bestowed on him the nickname "Uncle Louie".

The Liberals reserved their greatest effort for a mass meeting in Toronto's Maple Leaf Gardens on the last Friday of the campaign. On hand were Walter Harris, aware that he would likely be defeated personally but putting on a bold front, C. D. Howe, in trouble in his riding as well, L. B. Pearson, Paul Hellyer, and a stage full of other party dignitaries. Over ten thousand people were packed into the sports stadium, and a sea of red and white photographs of the Prime Minister, fixed on sticks, waved gaily as he mounted onto the platform. There was some booing, but it only added spice to what seemed certain to be a happy evening. Howe, Harris, and Hellyer spoke first, then St. Laurent advanced to the microphone. He had just begun to hit his stride when a fifteen-year-old lad stepped out of the crowd with a poster, bearing the Prime Minister's picture, in his hand, walked a dozen steps up to the podium, muttered a few unintelligible words, and tore up the poster before St. Laurent's face. The seventy-five-year-old leader stared, open-mouthed and uncomprehending, at the spectacle; the crowd watched in hushed silence. Then the chairman of the meeting, fearing an attack on the Prime Minister, rushed forward to seize the wrongdoer; he only succeeded in pushing him backwards, and the boy fell down the steps, striking his head on the cement floor, and knocking himself unconscious. A horrified gasp rose from the crowd as the figure lay, crumpled and alone, a few feet below the Prime Minister of Canada. St. Laurent continued to stare at the scene as if in a state of shock. In a matter of a few seconds, which seemed like hours, the young man was surrounded by attendants, and within a few minutes he was able to stand up and be escorted out of the hall.

The first reaction over, the crowd turned its indignation upon the men on the platform; the incident appeared to prove the charges of the other parties that the Liberal oligarchy was so remote from the people that it could not be approached with impunity. As soon as the disorder had subsided sufficiently, St. Laurent resumed his speech, referring in a tone of regret to the 'unfortunate incident', provoked by the 'ill-advised youth', but he too was clearly shaken and was unable to regain his earlier enthusiasm. The crowd, for its part, was no longer interested in his remarks; all minds were on the lad, and wondering what was the extent of his injury. He had stolen the Prime Minister's final show.

From *Louis St. Laurent — Canadian* by Dale Thomson

John G. Diefenbaker

Mr. Diefenbaker, nicknamed "DIEF THE CHIEF" *because of his forceful style, is one of the outstanding platform personalities of this century. In the late fifties his oratory caught the imagination of the Canadian people, and in 1958 he led the Progressive Conservative Party to the biggest victory ever obtained in a federal election. The following paragraphs give a graphic, behind-the-scenes description of Mr. Diefenbaker in action on the campaign trail.*

The Chief put everything into a speech. When he came from the platform, he was dripping with perspiration like a boxer or baseball pitcher after a hard workout. Guthrie, Gilbert or I always stood ready with a clean shirt, heavy sweater, muffler and towel in an attaché case. Backstage, the Chief removed his soaking shirt and undershirt, towelled down and put on the dry shirt and sweater topped by the muffler. All this gave him the rakish air of an old-time bare-knuckle pro about to do roadwork.

Whistle-stopping kept everyone busy. The Chief and Mrs. Diefenbaker would be surrounded by a milling crowd on the station platform; a band would strike up; local dignitaries would come to the microphone and then the Chief would speak. Later, he would move among the crowds of people, a handshake and a word for each one; after this ritual, we'd move on to the next stop, twenty minutes or half an hour away. Before dinner, the Chief usually tried to lie down for an hour or so, working on his speech for the evening in a relaxed posture, glasses on the end of his nose, in a blizzard of notes. The Chief needed plenty of working room; nothing could be discarded or mislaid in the litter of papers, because the missing piece would inevitably turn out to be essential to the speech. When he wanted facts or figures, Guthrie and I made our way to the research room, carefully edging around the Chief's travelling lectern, standing there like an Egyptian sarcophagus, and went through the Hansard reports, newspaper clippings and other material until we found what we wanted. Sometimes we were successful.

The Chief's lectern occasioned almost endless difficulty. It was a large, unwieldy wooden stand, specially built so that the Chief would have a place to lay his notes while speaking. He did not like strange lecterns, because the lectern inevitably became a part of the performance; and confronted with a lectern which might be wobbly, short, or pitched at too steep an angle, the Chief was overcome with frustration. With his own lectern, however, he was at ease. He leaned on it, shuffled his papers, walked around it and generally used it as a theatrical prop. It was one of our jobs to see to it that when the Chief spoke, the lectern was in place. It was endlessly being carried off or on the train, with the help of local assistance; and often, when borne aboard late at night, its coffin-like appearance must have caused spectators to wonder whether the campaign had been marred by untimely tragedy.

From *The Chief* by Thomas Van Dusen

Lester B. Pearson

In contrast to Mr. Diefenbaker's vigorous style was the gentle approach of Lester Bowles Pearson. This former diplomat, the only Canadian to receive the Nobel Prize for world peace, was Prime Minister during Canada's centennial year.

Liberal leader Lester B. Pearson encountered his share of unexpected incidents. He was visiting an elderly people's home in Nova Scotia one morning when a tiny, wizened woman came over to shake his hand. She stuck an envelope in his coat pocket. Later, when one of his secretaries opened it, she found a dollar bill inside. Scribbled on a note were these words, "To help you lick those Tories." It brought tears to Pearson's eyes.

From *Assignment Ottawa* by Peter Dempson

Pierre Elliott Trudeau

When Pierre Elliott Trudeau was elected leader of the Liberal party in 1967, Canadians met a colourful and controversial new leader.

In his first formal campaigning — a swing through metro Toronto — he discovered the ideal forum for what Dalton Camp called "a non-campaign": the shopping plaza. But although his opponents derided him as Pierre de la Plaza, there was nothing wrong in itself in his going where the people were, to plazas, parks, and city hall steps, "finding the people who [were] not committed and [wouldn't] go to a rally in the evening because it [was] miles away from the suburb in which they [lived]." Largely abandoning the concept of the formal meeting, he sped across the country in a DC-9 jet — thus reinforcing his modern, glamorous image — sometimes visiting three provinces in one day. By using helicopters to reach small centres, he created "the anticipatory excitement of a god descending from the sun into the midst of his people .... This is the jet age, man. And there is the jet age candidate."

From *Pendulum of Power* by J. M. Beck

QUESTIONS

1. Summarize what you feel was the main strength or weakness of each of the famous Canadian campaigners discussed in this chapter.
2. Choose a contemporary political figure in Canada and summarize what you consider to be his or her campaign style.
How does his or her style compare with the styles of the historical campaigners about whom you have read?
3. In what ways have the technological developments of the twentieth century affected election campaigns?
How would you picture campaigns of the future being different from those of today?
4. Prepare to debate one side of the proposition, "Campaign styles are more important than campaign issues."

5/The image makers

"A Person You Can Trust" is an ideal slogan for a car salesman, a funeral director or a politician. In fact it is a slogan you often hear associated with each of these. Their services differ greatly, but they share the common problem of having to attract public attention and gain public support.

In all three cases, campaigns handled by publicity specialists, called public relations people, may be carefully planned to gain this vital attention and support. In other words, a political figure is as eager to create a favourable public image as anyone in business. If people like the way they see you, they will support you.

What political leaders in your own area seem to you to have created a favourable public image?

How have they accomplished this?

What factors besides his public image should determine our support for a political figure?

"... we feel our strongest campaign stategy is to present him as the least of all the evils..."

The 1972 election: a case study

When Canadians voted in the federal election of 1972 the images of the two major party leaders differed greatly. Here are two articles which summarize their contrasting styles. As you read these, watch for the differences in their images.

Pierre Elliott Trudeau

Style is as hard to define as sex appeal, but Mr. Trudeau has it, compounded of physical appearance, manner of dress, illuminating intelligence and a score of other ingredients, many of them, no doubt, myths, but none the less important.

The engaging face, with its high cheek-bones, interesting creases, lively eyes and mobile mouth, the Mercedes sports car, ascot ties and sandals. The racy reputation as wealthy bachelor surrounded by beautiful women. The academic achievements at some of the world's best universities. The judo brown belt, the acquaintance with yoga. The world traveller who was once arrested by Arabs as an Israeli spy. The crusading intellectual who campaigned against Duplessis, helped launch Quebec's Quiet Revolution, went to work as a trade union adviser in the struggle for social justice, opposed nuclear arms in 1963, and has now become the leading champion of federalism against nationalism in Quebec.

All this and more goes to create the Trudeau style, appealing to many women and attractive to most men. In a sense, he is the man we would all like to be: charming, rich, talented, successful.

From "Is charisma the key to solving the Trudeau mystery" by Anthony Westell, *The Globe and Mail,* February 12, 1968

Robert Lorne Stanfield

His eyebrows are as bushy as ever, scraggly brush clinging to the precipice of a brow, but his fingernails are always manicured. One bit of advice he has accepted is to wear lighter suits so as not to appear too forbidding on television.

[As a public speaker] he has improved, mainly because he speaks faster and with more assurance, but the overall impression is too much caution, too dull.

Social Credit leader, Real Caouette probably expressed fears of ardent Tories when he said this year, the Conservatives lose 10,000 votes every time Mr. Stanfield goes on television.

One of the funniest Stanfield exchanges on television was on a hotline show in Hamilton and a caller persistently muddled his name — "Mr. Stanbury?" — until he reacted almost plaintively: "Stanfield's my name and it's my birthday. Surely you can remember my name on my birthday."

His weaknesses as a politician would be a litany of virtues in any other profession: honesty, trust, reliability, integrity. But they are old words. He is basically a likeable, very decent man, but not visceral at all. One senses, in an alley, he would go after an opponent with a cricket bat instead of a knife.

In the dark, cavernous fabrication shop at the Dartmouth shipyards last week, Mr. Stanfield roamed with his entourage, stopping to chat and shake hands with grimy men. The only sparks came from the welder's torches. He never causes much of a commotion.

"I call him Mr. Integrity," said Ted Cleave, Mr. Stanfield's campaign manager in Halifax. We were walking about 15 feet behind the entourage. "He's honest, sincere, able . . ."

"But does that win votes?" he was asked.

"Regrettably, it doesn't."

From "Stanfield: an image of trivia and cliché" by Martin O'Malley, *The Globe and Mail*, May 4, 1972

Fuddle-duddle vs. Fuddy-duddy

Redesigning Robert: an exercise in political image-making

QUESTIONS

1. Compose a chart in which you contrast the images of these two men.
2. To what types of voters would each style be appealing?
3. Would you feel comfortable supporting a potential Prime Minister on the basis of this information? What other kinds of information would you want to know?

Maclean's magazine asked a noted hair stylist, Christopher Beacom, to remake the image of Robert Stanfield by suggesting ways to alter his appearance. Here are Mr. Beacom's comments. The retouched photographs which follow show two of Mr. Beacom's attempts at restyling the Stanfield image.

Robert Stanfield is the example of a man who has strong characteristics that he has not yet taken advantage of. In fact his dogmatic, conservative, almost upper-class British image doesn't do his political positions justice. The high forehead caused by balding is distracting on camera (a light reflection always seems to bounce off one side causing the viewer to lose concentration on what he's saying). The bushy eyebrows are too severe and don't lend themselves to natural expression. The nose and chin are, therefore, too dominating. The clothes accentuate his severity. The problem is to soften his hard image and make his personality more appealing.

From *Maclean's,* May 1972

The real Robert Stanfield

The Beacom Stanfield, Mark I

The Beacom Stanfield, Mark II

QUESTIONS

1. Describe the alterations made to Mr. Stanfield's appearance in each of the preceding pictures. How do these changes affect your feelings towards Mr. Stanfield?

2. How would you expect each "new" Mr. Stanfield to behave on television, in front of a campaign crowd, or as a leader of Canada?

3. In 1969 Mr. Stanfield said, "You are what you are, and I am what I am. I can't change except to a limited degree without becoming a phony."

If you were to advise Mr. Stanfield on his public image would you respect his opinion or would you urge him to consider Mr. Beacom's suggestions?

4. It appears that the image of a candidate can be manipulated so that the public may not see the true type of individual for whom they are voting. How can voters see through a public relations image to assess the essential qualities of a leader?

6/The backroom boys

Canada's first Prime Minister once said that, to win an election, a candidate needs more than prayers. He needs a good organization, and to create this he needs a good source of money.

Some of the most important, but often unanswered, questions about elections concern finances.

Who pays?

How much does campaigning cost?

Do contributors get special favours?

The following items attempt to present some answers to questions such as these.

There are only two major sources of campaign money in this country. These sources are: (a) big business and (b) big unions.

On one occasion I was asked to see the top executive of a corporation who not only could withhold a large donation from his own firm but also could influence other major donating corporations. My task was to convince him that our party was going to win the election, that we had a common interest in the development of Canada and that the party had the right men and the right policies to do the job properly.

It must have been all right because at the end of two hours he said, ''Tell Mr. ----- (our collector in that province) to stop in to see me next week.'' But two days later, he called me in a rage because in the interval our party had taken a stand in the House of Commons on a problem which, he said, showed we were ''toadying to organized labour.'' ''There will be no need for Mr. ----- to call on me,'' he concluded.

In that instance, the party did not change its stand and the tycoon simmered but not before he had tried his best to change our policy.

From ''For the sake of argument'' by J. Scott, *Maclean's,* September 9, 1961

Trials and tribulations of fund raising—No. 2

In February, 1972 the Liberal Party announced the creation of a money-raising scheme called the Red Carnation Fund. Some people speculated that its name came from the flowers the party leader, Mr. Trudeau, liked to wear in his lapel.

Mr. Bob Rankin was one of the fund's workers. He is speaking with Michael Woodward, a reporter for CFPL-TV, *London.*

Woodward: How do you go about raising money on the corporate campaign trail?

Rankin: Usually through personal contact.

Woodward: You mean people you know personally?

Rankin: That I know personally.

Woodward: How do you put the arm on them?

Rankin: Ha! I never put the arm on anyone, Mike. I usually write and try and seek an appointment and discuss our objectives in the election campaign. The objective of not only the funds and the expenses involved but the objective of the party.

Woodward: Are there ever any strings attached to the kind of money you get from corporate donations?

Rankin: Never! I've made it consistently clear that the Liberal Party is not and never has been for sale ...

Woodward: How do you feel about full disclosure of where political funds come from?

Rankin: Mixed emotions, Mike. I'm not absolutely against it and I don't think many of the donors are either. There are some people who feel that the amount they give and to whom they give it is their business and they don't want it disclosed.

And it is their business really.

Others really couldn't care less.

So it's kind of a mixed bag.

The biggest fear, I think, that the corporations have in making donations is one of the motive behind it, that the motive will be mistaken and will be taken as some kind of patronage gift to the party. Which is the furthest thing from the truth.

Woodward: Have you ever discussed corporate contributions with one of these donors to find out how they feel about their motives?

Rankin: Yes, of course, I discuss it with them on the collection effort that I've made ... I think corporations and the people at large are wanting to participate. They seem willing, more willing than in previous years that I've been involved ... to give in the interests of the two-party political system, the two major parties.

I'm not knocking the NDP by saying that, but my experience is with the Liberal Party and I think this is what they find too, that people are interested in contributing in the interest of good government.

Woodward: Why do you think that industrial and commercial interests are anxious to maintain what you call good government? What would you define as good government?

Rankin: I think good government is a free enterprise system; that's what they're interested in maintaining. And they're interested in maintaining good candidates, a good quality of government and quality programs of government.

Woodward: ... Isn't there any possibility of pressure brought to bear by corporate donors after an election to suppress certain kinds of legislation, to promote other kinds of legislation, to take it easy on tax reform?

Rankin: There's always that possibility, Mike, but certainly I wouldn't be part of it and I don't think anyone else in the Liberal Party would be.

I have found that essentially getting funds for elections and to maintain the party between elections with our Red Carnation Fund is a real selling job. These people aren't giving money to get favours; they're giving money in the interests of good government.

Trials and tribulations of fund raising—No. 3

Woodward: If their motives in making these contributions are liable to suspicion, how about the motives of the Liberal Party in accepting these corporate contributions?

Rankin: Well, heavens, Mike, the Liberal Party has to exist. We have to pay a staff, albeit a small one. We publish a party newspaper on a monthly basis, and it has to be paid for. There are many functions of the Party that have to be maintained by a fund of some kind or another. And we have to raise this money, in my case . . . in amounts of five dollars to five hundred dollars. And I might say there are a lot more five dollars than five hundred dollars.

from "Politics: Where The Money Comes From," CFPL-TV, London, Ontario

A brief look at the New Democrats and Socreds shows that, at the federal level at least, their financing is much more open and responsible, perhaps for the good reason that neither party has anything much to sell in the way of public preferment. Anyone who has ever belonged to the CCF or NDP — as I have — knows that every meeting is marked by the passing of a hat, the sale of subscriptions, literature, books, raffle tickets, and so forth. Socred meetings tend to be much the same. These hat-passing routines, along with annual memberships, bake sales, suppers and special fund drives, provide the on-going funds for the two smaller parties. (The two old-line parties get their money in big chunks at election time and spread it out over the lean years between elections.)

In addition, the NDP has a "check-off" system under which unions can vote to affiliate themselves to the party. When this happens, the members of the affiliated local are required to donate to the party five cents per month, which is automatically deducted from their pay. Any union member who disagrees may, even if his local has voted to affiliate, sign a form exempting himself, and thus be relieved of the obligation. This check-off provides the second most important source of revenue for the party. (The NDP's public statement of revenues and expenditures shows that in 1972, of total revenues of $205,181 received at the federal level, memberships provided $102,116 and affiliated membership $89,229.) It is, nonetheless, a bum idea. The NDP defence of the arrangement comes down to the fact that the party would be hamstrung without it — to which any Liberal or Tory might reply that his party, too, would be crippled by having to give up corporate handouts. To the argument that the check-off system compels men and women who don't like the NDP to support it, the party replies that it would be much more costly and complicated to require members to sign in to the check-off, instead of to sign out, and that in any event the option is there for any who do not wish to donate. In fact, the union member who begs off is conspicuous to the union officers, who are often on the local NDP executive; and the pressure to stay enrolled is exactly as oppressive, though not nearly so financially rewarding to the party, as the veiled threat to corporations that they should kick in to Liberal and Tory coffers if they know what's good for them.

Union pledges *do* buy influence with the party. In the spring of 1972, when the Waffle split was boiling up through NDP ranks, it was a private meeting of key union leaders — Bill Mahoney of the Steelworkers, Dennis McDermott of the United Auto Workers, and others — with David and Stephen Lewis that brought the matter to a head. The Union Leaders told the Lewises that their union memberships were being upset by the battle and that their own leadership was under attack, and they damn well wanted the Waffle mess cleared up. They did not threaten to withdraw financial aid (although the president of a Hamilton Steelworkers' local did make such a threat to Robert MacKenzie, a Steelworkers' representative and NDP candidate), but the message could hardly have been clearer. Well, the Steelworkers and the United Auto Workers represent between them more than half of all the affiliated members in the NDP (the party's confidential records show 277,469 affiliated members as of April 1, 1973; of these, 86,208 belong to the Steelworkers and 72,405 to the UAW), and the pressure of that meeting was what lay behind the attack launched on the Waffle soon afterwards by Stephen Lewis.

These union donations also help to explain the way the NDP has softpedalled the nationalist issue; most of the unions who provide half the party funding are international — for which read, U.S. — organizations; some of them are autonomous and some are not, but none of them is anxious to pursue the issue of economic nationalism, and their influence is felt by the party right where it counts — in the pocket book.

From *Divide and Con* by Walter Stewart

QUESTIONS

1. It appears that fewer than 5% of all Canadian voters have ever contributed to the finances of our political parties. Why have Canadians been so reluctant to make contributions?

2. Finding money to run their campaigns has always been a problem for party directors, and sometimes this has led to scandals. Investigate one such scandal as the Pacific Scandal (1870's) or the Beauharnois Affair (1920's).

3. If you were interviewing applicants for the job of fund-raiser for a party, what qualities would you be seeking in the person you select? Why are women apparently seldom used in this role?

4. In the first of these articles Mr. Scott says there are two sources from which a party can get money — big business and big unions.

   (a) What are the advantages and the disadvantages of using each source?

   (b) How would the sources each party depends on reflect that party's basic approach to political ideas?

5. Canadians who make donations to political parties may deduct part of these donations from their taxable income.

   (a) By referring to the current Guide Book for the Canadian income tax, find out how this plan works and the ways in which taxpayers can make use of it.

   (b) In your opinion, what are the motives for this plan? What are its advantages likely to be for our nation?

The election expenses act

On January 3, 1974, the House of Commons completed debate on Bill C203, a scheme to regulate campaign spending. This was called the Election Expenses Act.

The law now states:

* In his riding a candidate may only spend up to $1 for each of the first 15,000 voters, 50¢ for each of the next 10,000 voters, and 25¢ for all other voters.
* A national party organization may spend up to 30¢ for each voter.
* Part of a candidate's expenses for travelling, postage and the auditing of his finances will be covered by money raised through taxes.
* The names of donors who give more than $100 must be made public.
* Radio and TV stations must distribute some free time for broadcasts among the political parties.
* Those who fail to abide by these rules may be penalized up to $25,000.

QUESTION

1. The critics of the Election Expenses Act seem to have three basic points of opposition. They say it isn't equally fair to all parties; it isn't fair to taxpayers; it isn't fair to donors.

(a) What are the grounds to support each criticism?

(b) What is your own stand on the merit of Bill C203?

Election spending: a comparison

1972 election, Conservative Party spending

Media advertising	$1,300,000
Leader's tour	150,000
Riding support	1,600,000
Administration	400,000
Campaign aid	300,000
Voter research	100,000
	$3,850,000

1972 election, NDP spending

Deposits ($200 per candidate)	$ 14,400
Organization	57,475
Travel — organizers	11,460
Telephone, telegraph, postage	8,654
Printing (less sales of $55,806)	11,768
Leader's tour	23,632
Survey (part of a Gallup poll)	12,012
Contingencies (extra staff and bad debts)	12,014
Media	163,423
	$ 314,838

From *Divide and Con* by Walter Stewart

Case study: Peter Maloney lost an election, and that's not all

Peter Maloney decided it was his civic duty, so he stood as a candidate in last October's Ontario provincial election. But all he succeeded in doing was driving himself irredeemably into debt. His publicly declared bankruptcy reveals his campaign costs almost dollar for dollar, and provides a rare lesson about what the game of politics can do to a man of modest means.

Less than a year ago, Maloney was living the life that could be expected of a clever, 26-year-old bachelor. He was a $14,000-a-year economist at the Toronto Stock Exchange. He lived in a $275-a-month downtown Toronto apartment, he dressed well, he entertained a lot and he always had more than a few dollars in his pocket.

He was generous, and especially interested in bailing out teenagers in trouble — at whatever cost to himself. Once he flew to Vancouver just to help two youths who, it appeared, were about to be unfairly charged as accessories to the theft of some credit cards. Maloney convinced police the youths were innocent, then he paid for their flight back to Toronto. That weekend cost him nearly $1,000.

Then Maloney won the Liberal nomination in the central Toronto riding of St. George, and ran against the popular and powerful Allan Lawrence, the attorney-general who had almost won the Conservative party leadership from William Davis. Lawrence beat Maloney by 9,492 votes.

Today Maloney rents a small, sparsely-furnished, $100-a-month room in one of the grubbier sections of Toronto. He doesn't entertain at all and the pockets of his remaining good suit are usually empty. He certainly has no money for kids in trouble with the law.

What he does have are 56 creditors, including two banks, two finance companies, a hardware store, a printing shop, a lumberyard and a couple of utility companies, who are demanding payment of bills he ran up during his campaign (the final tally is not yet in, but will exceed $15,000).

The rest of his total $30,000-plus bankruptcy consists of Maloney's personal, non-campaign debts piled up at university, and in setting up previous homes in Ottawa and Toronto.

Maloney filed bankruptcy in December last year when his lawyer told him just how badly off he was.

"I guess I really didn't understand all a political campaign entailed," Maloney says. "It was a whole new experience. The worst part of it is that I don't think you ever really recover from a bankruptcy.

"It's like a criminal record — only in financial terms. You never get over it. I hope someday to be well enough off to pay these people in full. That's the only real way out."

A person who declares bankruptcy in Canada does not merely sell off all his assets, distribute the money among his creditors as far as it will go, and then start fresh. When Maloney's bankruptcy gets to court later this year, his creditors will be there asking for a portion of Maloney's future earnings. They'll never get all their money (such are the perils of giving credit) but the judge will likely decide Maloney can reasonably be expected to pay between 15 and 20 cents on each dollar he owes. Then the judge will decide how long Maloney can have to pay up. The judge will consider that Maloney must be left with enough income to maintain a standard of living appropriate to his job (he'll need another suit, for instance).

Maloney will have to pay a fixed regular sum into the court, which will distribute it among his creditors. Only when the agreed percentage is paid will Maloney be discharged from the obligation of the bankruptcy. "I can only hope," says Maloney, "that it won't leave me completely broke." The Maloney campaign was comparatively modest and inexpensive.

He secured the St. George nomination on Feb. 22 last year, and in March hired a 27-year-old research assistant, Kathy Jones, at $115 a week. The Liberal party organization promised it would give Maloney an unspecified amount after the election had been formally declared. Meanwhile, Miss Jones began writing and phoning everyone in the riding who might be sympathetic enough to make a contribution. "We started from scratch," says Maloney. "We didn't even have a list of party members or any indication of where the riding's Liberal supporters were located."

Since there was no Liberal party money available when Miss Jones was hired, Maloney paid her himself, and she worked out of her home (Miss Jones eventually agreed to work for no pay at all).

By June, some cheques began arriving. Maloney reckons that about five per cent of the people he approached sent in contributions that totalled about $3,000. As well, $1,800 finally came in from the St. George Riding Liberal Association.

"Kathy's initial success was so encouraging that I really never thought we'd have money trouble," Maloney says. "I didn't really think about it at all then."

With the fresh funds, Maloney rented a small, $130-a-month office, and outfitted it for work. He borrowed furniture from his church, and even managed to borrow a Gestetner copying machine. But necessary equipment that he had to rent began to cut into the money. Painting and drapes for the office ran to almost $100, an air conditioner cost $125 a month. Bulletin boards cost $20. Two IBM typewriters at $22 a month were needed as well as a postage machine, pens, pencils, stationery, thumbtacks, scissors, stencils, typewriter ribbons, note pads, staplers and paper clips.

To get publicity, a grand opening of the new office was held, with all the Liberals in the area invited, including leader Robert Nixon. "Nobody knew who I was at first," Maloney says. "We needed some kind of spectacular happening to attract the press and people who might be interested in working as volunteers in the campaign." He hired a rock band for $300, and 200 guests consumed about $100 worth of wine and $35 worth of cheese. When it was over, the newspapers knew

who Peter Maloney was — and touted him as the giant-killer who could beat Allan Lawrence. But Maloney's funds were almost gone.

Over the summer, there was enough money left for a few wine and cheese parties at some of the many nursing homes in the riding, and to carry on the mailings to potential supporters, but by September, when the election was at last announced and the official campaign got underway, the Maloney campaign was broke except for $1,000 that finally arrived from the provincial Liberal association.

An attempt to raise funds at a dance earlier in August had proved disastrous. About six cases of liquor worth almost $300 were stolen from the church basement, and the receipts from the cash register also came out short because somebody's hand had been in the till. As a result of the thefts, the dance lost about $200.

To add to the troubles, Kathy Jones, the campaign's only fund raiser, got mononucleosis and was out of action for more than a month. And in mid-August Maloney had taken leave without pay from his stock exchange job until the end of the campaign.

But somehow he had to have hundreds of signs printed, at 40¢ a sign, and he needed more literature printed and distributed. A Liberal supporter offered a free office nearby which had to be cleaned and painted, and the furniture and supplies had to be moved by leased truck from the old office. "By this time I was financing the whole campaign on credit," says Maloney. "There was just no money."

Maloney had not paid the rent on his apartment for two months, and an eviction notice ordered him out by the end of October — a week after the election. He moved, and he still owes his landlord, Greenwin Property Management, $795.

The candidate put himself on a $5-a-day living allowance. "I was able to have my 90-cent bacon and egg breakfast at the Maple Leaf Open Kitchen," he recalls.

	Minimum		1st Option		2nd Option				
	Estimated	Actual	Estimated	Actual					
HEADQUARTERS									
Committee Rooms									
Office Manager									
Telephone									
Furniture & Equip									
(Not Donated -									
begged borrowed or stolen)									
Insurance (Liability									
Fire)									
Office Supplies, Staples,									
Stationery & Coffee, etc.	xxx								
CAMPAIGN MANAGER									
(If Paid)	xxx								
CANDIDATES TRAVEL EXPENSE	xxx								
ADVERTISING &									
PUBLICITY									
Signs									
Large Masonite									
Lawn & Window			Additional Signs xxx							
Metal Stakes			Signs & Stakes							
Wood Stakes									
* Billboards									
Canvass pamphlet									
(Art Work & Printing)									
MEDIA									
Radio, Tv &			Additional	xxx	Additional	xxx				
Newspapers			Advertising		Advertising					
Photos & Plates									
(In Large Urban Centres									
put this money into									
following options)	xxx								
Additional pieces -			Postal Mail Drop xxx		Direct Mail Letter	xxx				
pamphlet or newspaper			(In minimum budget,		to uncommitted voters					
"U-Vote-Ats"			pamphlet was budgeted		in new sub division)					
			for hand delivery. If							
			funds are available, use							
Direct Mailings to select groups			postal drop)							
ELECTION NIGHT									
EXPENSES	xxx								
SPECIAL EVENTS									
RALLIES	xxx								
TOTALS	$ xxx		xxx		xxx					

To help candidates control their spending, the Liberal party distributed campaign expense sheets, like the one above, to every one of its constituency headquarters in the 1974 federal election.

Toward the end of September Maloney asked his mother to help with the campaign. "She moved into my apartment and began buying groceries so I'd eat properly," Maloney says. "By this time, of course, I knew we were in deep financial trouble, but there was nothing to do but keep going. Things started to look encouraging in the press, and I realized I was committed to the end no matter what.

"I had to keep going despite the money because of the people who were depending on me to put across their points of view. I had gone to rate-payers' groups, in fact all the organizations I could honestly align myself with, and I had told them that if they voted for me I would represent them. There was a definite obligation by then." I was in St. George riding at election time and there was indeed a feeling toward the end of the campaign that Maloney just might knock off Allan Lawrence, the Number 2 man in the Ontario cabinet.

During the last week of the campaign, the Liberal party kicked in another $1,500 because of the ob-viously effective campaign being waged. "But it was just too late," says Maloney. And after election day, the bills started coming in.

"We tried some post-election fund-raising, but drew a blank," Maloney says. "Nobody is interested in bailing out a loser. I suppose if I had won, Liberals would not have allowed their sitting member to be embarrassed with a bankruptcy, but that's the price of losing."

Maloney returned to his job as assistant to the vice-president of market research at the stock exchange and began trying to pay off the debts. "My salary was being perpetually garnisheed, making things intolerable."

He retained a lawyer for $100 and was advised to turn his affairs over to a trustee. Bankruptcies in Canada must be administered by a chartered accountant who is licensed as a trustee. Maloney's financial affairs are now administered by Harris, Title, Grossman and Co.

When Peter Maloney talks about those days last fall, when he and his friends pounded on doors and collared people at shopping plazas from 5 a.m. to past midnight, he smiles and his voice takes on an excited edge. "It was really something," he says. "We felt so with it. We were the underdogs. Us against the world. So many good things happened. So many people helped and worked for nothing and we met so many people.

"My real regret," he says wistfully, "is that I will have to wait years before I can run again."

From "Peter Maloney lost an election" by Hartley Steward, *The Canadian Magazine*, March 11, 1972

QUESTIONS

1. To what degree does the article about Peter Maloney support the theory that politics is a game for the rich?
2. To what degree did Peter Maloney's participa-tion in politics and to what degree did his own decisions bankrupt him?
3. In your opinion how would Bill C203 have helped Peter Maloney's plight?
4. If you were Peter Maloney would you regret or cherish your election experience? Why?
5. Appoint a class committee to seek out a local politician who is willing to discuss with you the finances of his campaigns. Prepare in advance the questions you will pose to him, using the campaign expense sheet on the preceding page as a guide.

7/Elections

WHO RUNS THE ELECTION TO BE SURE ALL THE VOTING IS FAIR?

The nation must be prepared at any time to hold an election involving the House of Commons. The government maintains an office and a staff in Ottawa who are constantly able to supervise elections.

This bureau is called the Office of the Chief Electoral Officer. It was first established in 1920 and it has directed each general election since that time.

Whenever the Chief Electoral Officer is informed that the Governor General has officially dissolved or ended one Parliament and issued orders for a new one to be elected, he immediately begins plans to run the election.

The Chief Electoral Officer is responsible for all that occurs during the voting. To help him with this task he appoints an official for each riding. This person is called the Returning Officer, and it is his job to direct the election in that one constituency.

The Returning Officers work to divide the territory of their ridings into very small sections so that the voters will not have far to go when they vote. Each of these sections is called a poll. In each poll the Returning Officer finds a home, a school, a church basement, a hall or some other place where the district voters can come.

The Returning Officer also appoints a resident to control the election in each poll. That official is called a Deputy Returning Officer and he may have one or two poll clerks to assist him. The poll may also have a citizen who acts as a law officer to be sure that all the proceedings are correctly carried on.

Each of these jobs — the Deputy Returning Officer's, the poll clerks', the law officer's — lasts only one day, but each person is paid for his work on that day. The Returning Officer's position may extend over several months both before and after the election.

With an organization like this the Chief Electoral Officer covers every single spot in Canada. The nation is ready to vote.

The voters select an MP for each of the two hundred and sixty-four constituencies across the country. This is called a general or federal election.

Sometimes the Chief Electoral Officer must prepare for a by-election, an election in just one riding. A by-election occurs when a single seat in the House of Commons is vacant, perhaps because of the death of an MP or his resignation from the House to take another position.

By-elections occur between general elections. Although they do not require as much work from the Chief Electoral Officer and his staff, they do show why there is a permanent need for such an official.

WHO CAN VOTE? WHO CAN'T VOTE?

Long before voting day the Returning Officer in each constituency hires citizens to compile a list of voters. These workers are called enumerators and the results of their work are posted on tree trunks, telephone poles, and the sides of public buildings throughout the riding weeks before the election. Each citizen must check the Voters' List to be sure his name is recorded there.

The vote, called the franchise, is for every Canadian citizen eighteen years of age or older.

Canadian law does deny some citizens the right to cast a ballot. The Chief Electoral Officer and his Assistant in Ottawa cannot vote. Judges appointed by the Federal government cannot vote. A Returning Officer may vote only in the case of a tie in his riding.

Persons serving punishment for breaking the law are also denied the franchise. People in mental institutions lose their right to vote. Anyone who has been convicted of an illegal act involving an election also faces the same loss.

HOW CAN WE BE SURE EACH CANDIDATE IS SERIOUS ABOUT THE JOB?

At a certain time and place announced by the Chief Electoral Officer and the Returning Officer of a riding, the names of citizens who want to run for the position of Member of Parliament will be accepted.

When a party submits its candidate's name with the signatures of twenty-five voters who nominate him, it must also make a payment of two hundred dollars called the electoral deposit.

This deposit is required to act as a safeguard for the voters. Such an amount of money is not so much that it would keep a serious candidate from running in the election. Yet it is too much money for a "joker" to throw away just for the chance to see his name on the ballot. The electoral deposit is really a way of having only serious candidates run for election.

Following the voting, the winner gets his deposit back. Any other candidate who received at least half as many votes as the winner also gets back his deposit.

When the polls close every candidate is allowed to have representatives who watch for problems in the ballot counting. These people are called scrutineers; no more than one scrutineer per candidate is permitted in a polling division. Scrutineers can also act as communicators to relay the results of the vote back to their party headquarters. If they do their job properly the party organization will know the results of the election perhaps even before the Returning Officer officially hears from his Deputies.

VICTORY — Otto Jelinek, 1974

DEFEAT — David Lewis, 1974

Sunday	Monday	Tuesday	Wednesday	Th
	56 May 13 Contact supporters to see whether they own properties with large billboards or wall space where it's possible to place *big* signs	**55 May 14** Send out news story to local press. TV, radio stations. Be sure to include pictures	**54 May 15** Urban enumerators must be nominated. Plan your signs, posters, brochures, media campaign if you haven't already done so	**53** Deputy bases a one is dresse outside
50 May 19 Have a campaign meeting with all committee chairmen	**49 May 20** Urban and rural enumeration begins.	**48 May 21** List of revising agents should be prepared for the Returning Officer. Begin arrangements for radio and TV time, if you haven't already done so	**47 May 22** Check Returning Officers to see if "Special Voters Lists" are available for inspection. Arrange to obtain them from R.O. Begin first canvass survey	**46** Get yo arrang erty. S
43 May 26 Provincial Chairmen: Make sure nominations for D.R.O. and Scrutineers have been forwarded to National Headquarters.	**42 May 27** Enumerators preliminary lists of voters should be presented to Returning Officer and posted in the Polling Division.	**41 May 28** Get numerous copies of nomination papers from Returning Officer. Post prominently in committee room. Have all voter supporters sign, and witness signatures.	**40 May 29** Make sure first mailing of candidate and central information has gone out to "Special Voters." Lists of "Special Voters" must be posted at each R.O. Headquarters.	**39** You sh list from Begin candidi
36 June 2 Arrange a campaign committee meeting with all committee chairmen	**35 June 3** Take inventory of campaign literature and material. Are signs up? Are brochures and stickers distributed? Have you arranged for radio and/or TV time?	**34 June 4** Send out another news release, with pictures	**33 June 5** Check with Returning Officer on location of sittings for revision. Order your "Vote-At" cards from your printer. Have postal # imprinted. You must get these cards back within 7 days!	**32** Distri voters
29 June 9 Last day for candidates to give nomination of revising agents to Returning Officer. Have all voters present sign nomination papers. Remember to arrange for any paid radio and TV commercials and newspaper ads in your plan—but don't schedule too many too soon.	**28 June 10** Nomination Day for the 21 Electoral Districts in Schedule III (See foot note): last day to appoint official Agent. After checking all names, nomination papers—including party endorsement—must be filed with Returning Officer by today. Get a receipt and send telegram of confirmation to your Provincial chairman.	**27 June 11** Certain designated voters are allowed to vote by proxy. (For details, see Elections Act.) Appoint special Committee to follow this up.	**26 June 12** Printing of Voters Lists to be completed by today. Get at least 10 agent slips per poll from Returning Officer. Have candidate sign some every day.	**25** Last day of revisi
22 June 16 It's Sunday—work only half a day (12 hours) But be sure you meet with all committee chairmen	**21 June 17** Nomination Day! Your candidate *must* be nominated by 2:00 P.M. today or you have no candidate. And this is your last day to appoint an official Agent. After checking all names, nomination papers—including party endorsement—must be filed with Returning Officer by today. Get a receipt and send telegram of confirmation to your Provincial chairman.	**20 June 18** Check your supply of materials—signs, posters, brochures, badges, stickers, etc. Estimate whether additional supplies will be needed before Election-Day—and if "Yes", order now!	**19 June 19** First revision day for urban and rural electoral lists. Last day of rural list by enumerator	**18** Second Last day
15 June 23 Have a campaign meeting with all committee chairmen. Pay special attention to their reports of the areas that need "shoring up".	**14 June 24** "Special Voting" starts. In riding where Armed Forces bases are situated, scrutineers should be attending each "Special Vote Poll." Mail "Vote-At" cards to ensure delivery on time.	**13 June 25** Last day for objections to revised electoral list. If "Vote-At" cards are hand-delivered, you must start today to assure complete delivery.	**12 June 26** Arrange personal appearances—shopping plazas, plant gates, etc. Hand out stickers and literature personally, so voters will re-*member you.*	**11** Make s availabl paign.
8 June 30 Hold a committee meeting with all committee chairmen. Go over plans for final week in full detail—this is the week that most voters make up their minds!	**7 ADVANCE POLL 8 A.M.—8 P.M. July 1 MONDAY** Last day of Advance Polls—P.C. workers' final chance to vote before E-day.	**6 July 2** Arrange appearances on public service radio and television programs to discuss the issues	**5 July 3** "Special Vote" counting commences at each voting territory headquarters. Obtain a copy of each record of completed affidavits for voting at Advance Polls.	**4** Last "V by now spots s the-vot

1 July 7
Final day
Morning Hold meeting of all important E-Day chairmen.
Afternoon Gather all E-Day workers for final instruction.
Evening Get "doorhanger cards" out tonight

ELECTION DAY   July 8

Poll Captains: Be at your polls by 7:45 a.m.
Polling stations are open from 8:00 a.m. to 7:00 p.m.
Workers: Used marked voters list and get out *our* vote!
Counting of votes cast at Advance Polls at 9:00 p.m. At least one hour after polls close, "Special Vote" results given by Chief Electoral Officer by Returning Officer.

Schedule III (See Day 28)

Ontario	Manitoba	Newfoundland
Cochrane	Churchill	Bonavista—Trinity—Co
Kenora—Rainy River		Burin— Burgeo
Thunder Bay	**Saskatchewan**	Gander—Twillingate
	Mackenzie	Grand Falls—White Ba
Quebec	Meadow Lake	Humber—St. George's
Abitibi		
Manicouagan		

Published by the Progressive Conservative Party of Canada
Printed in Canada

candidate's calendar

	Friday	Saturday
y	**Friday**	**Saturday**

Friday

52 May 17
Meet with popular community leaders in various walks of life, and ask for their support. Have photographs taken with them, and send to newspapers.

45 May 24
Contact supporters to arrange coffee, tea, wine and cheese parties for you to attend. Remember: invite the uncommitted. Make sure plenty of campaign literature and other material is on hand.

38 May 31
If they're part of your Campaign, start erecting lawn, house, and window signs, and distributing bumper stickers.

31 June 7
Re-read **Winning Ways.**

24 June 14
Revising Agents commence their duties.

Get "Vote-At" cards prepared for area captains to deliver to homes of workers who are going to address them, if distribution is to be by mail.

17 June 21
Last day to get a voter on an urban voters list (third revision day).
"Special Voting Polls" must be established and published.

10 June 28
Send out a press release, make sure your final newspaper ads are ready, prepare any last-minute statements on the issues, gear up for the final push.

3 July 5
You must get proxy certificates by 10:00 a.m. today, and obtain transfer certificates and list of DRO's from Returning Officer.

Saturday

51 May 18
Contact printers, sign-makers and others to prepare your campaign material.

44 May 25
Last day for enumeration. Start preparing preliminary lists of electors. Remember to get a type-written copy of the enumerated "original" voters' lists.

37 June 1
Last day to begin first canvass/survey

30 June 8
Notice of holding of Advanced Polls must be published by Returning Officer.

23 June 15
Last day for Returning Officers to mail preliminary lists to urban electors.

Last day to begin second canvass/survey

16 June 22
Canvass homes, meet voters. Enlist your wife (or husband) and children to pass out your literature door-to-door—their support translates into votes.

9 ADVANCE POLL 8 A.M.–8 P.M. **June 29** SATURDAY
Day one of Advance Polls. All P.C.'s who will not be in own Poll on E-Day, should vote today!
"Special Voting" ends.
Last day to begin final canvass/survey.

2 July 6
Last day for cancellation of proxy certificates. "Special Vote" counting ends. Voters list must be marked by today.
Distribute agent slips to all E-Day workers

(left column, partial)

at Armed Forces d. Be sure some-names and ad-erans inside and fficer has names.

ommittee to work s on private prop-se.

eliminary electors cer.

stal walk" of

iterature and ask er you find them.

er to have notice

ban electoral list. withdraw.

paign literature is days of your cam-

uld be delivered ads, TV and radio d. Final "get-out-made.

rberta
hahasca
ace River
cky Mountain

ritish Columbia
ast Chilcotin
nce George—Peace River
eena

Yukon Territory
Yukon

Northwest Territories
Northwest Territories

For legal information call Legal Services.
P C Headquarters Ottawa
(613) 233-7711

Notes

_____

Progressive Conservative candidates used this calendar to help them organize the complex details of an election campaign.

Local campaigning

While the national party leaders get most of the publicity during an election campaign, it is actually the local candidates and their local campaigns which involve the greatest number of workers.

Case Study No. 1: A local election battle

Dartmouth-Halifax East is one of 264 constituencies where hundreds of party supporters actively campaigned for their candidates in 1972. A case study of this riding, written at the time of the campaign, reveals how elections are won and lost.

An escalating controversy over the proposed Ship Harbour national park is emerging as a volatile issue which threatens to overshadow an otherwise low-key campaign in the Dartmouth-Halifax East constituency.

A two-day swing through the riding indicated that national leadership is the central issue on the minds of most voters.

Liberal candidate Dr. John Savage, a Dartmouth physician who has been active in numerous community activities during the past five years, and Conservative candidate Mike Forrestall, who has represented the riding since 1965, clearly have the edge over NDP candidate Norman Dares.

Dares, a 22-year-old unemployed university graduate living with his parents in Dartmouth, admits the "odds are great" against his victory.

All three candidates agree that federal leadership is a big election issue in the riding, but each has a different version of its interpretation.

Mr. Forrestall claims the public has had enough of Pierre Trudeau and has realized that Robert Stanfield would restore responsible government.

Dr. Savage insists that Mr. Trudeau is easily the most effective national leader in the country, and that the "aura of infallibility" has been stripped from the PC leader to show a weak man.

Mr. Dares feels that David Lewis has strengthened the NDP, which offers the only long-term solution to the country's problems.

Dr. Savage and Mr. Forrestall are conducting the same style of campaign, while Mr. Dares is hampered by lack of workers and money.

The Liberal and Conservative style is the door-knocking, personal hand-shake method, with coffee parties scattered throughout and a tendency to avoid holding formal political rallies.

The Savage campaign has already involved the Prime Minister, the government leader in the Senate, Paul Martin, and Commons finance committee chairman Bob Kaplan, a Liberal MP from the Toronto riding of Don Valley. External Affairs Minister Mitchell Sharp will be in the riding later.

Mr. Forrestall says the presence of the Liberal "big guns" mirrors the party's desperation to win the seat.

His campaign has involved Dartmouth Mayor Roland Thornhill, provincial leader John Buchanan, and Hamilton West MP Lincoln Alexander, the only Negro in the Commons.

Both sides are making active use of the parties' youth wings in an attempt to capture the first-time vote, estimated at 21-25 per cent of the electorate.

The Savage campaign appears to rely heavily on morning coffee parties and occasional evening wine-and-cheese parties, similar to the style of the Dartmouth South provincial campaign in 1970 which elected Scott MacNutt.

There have been reports that the Liberal and Conservative campaigns cost between $40,000 and $50,000, but candidates on both sides scoff at this.

Mr. Dares' campaign pales by comparison.

He has pledges totalling $600 for his campaign. Of this amount $324 has already been spent to produce 20,000 campaign leaflets. Another $200 will go for his election deposit.

Mr. Dares does not own a car and has no driver's licence. His chief source of transportation is university student Klaus Jaunich, his official agent. But Mr. Jaunich must attend several morning classes, which hampers travel.

Mr. Dares is banking on a big vote from first-time voters.

The Dartmouth-Halifax East riding contains the Shearwater armed forces base, plus the naval armament depot in Dartmouth. The service vote, traditionally Liberal, almost split evenly in 1968, with 780 Liberal votes, 767 Conservative and 57 New Democrat.

Mr. Dares feels that the recent 10 per cent pay raise for armed forces personnel will attract a bigger Liberal vote, but Mr. Forrestall expects to do at least as well. (Campaigning on armed forces bases is not permitted.)

From "Leadership central issue in battle" by Peter Meerburg, *The Halifax Chronicle-Herald*, October 5, 1972

QUESTIONS

1. Using a chart compare the different issues, campaign methods, and financing of each party's candidate.
2. In such a local campaign, evaluate the roles of the party leaders and senior party members.
3. Based on the information of the case and other knowledge you have of Maritime politics, select the candidate who you think would win the election.
4. Research and prepare your own case study of the last federal election in your riding. Use the Dartmouth-Halifax East study as a model for your own project.

Case Study No. 2: Canvassing

As a guideline for its campaign workers a New Democratic Party organization published the following instructions.

QUESTIONS

1. What characteristics are the NDP directors obviously hoping their canvassers will demonstrate during the campaign?
2. Compile a class research record by interviewing relatives and friends who have stories to tell about interesting incidents from election campaigns which they remember.

How will I cast my ballot?

"The NDP's platform is designed for the working man's needs."

"The Social Credit tax proposal is bound to put more money in my pocket."

"The Liberals were the only party that cared enough to come three times to my door."

"The Conservatives have never done well in Quebec since Riel."

"Is the Liberal government really right when it says 'The land is strong'?"

"My grandfather and my father voted Conservative."

"What this country needs is the honesty and strong character of the NDP leader."

"Those Liberal ads on television were certainly well done."

"Am I throwing away my vote when the polls show the NDP cannot form a government?"

QUESTIONS

1. Each of these statements represents a factor or pressure which influences the voter's final decision. Give a title to each factor.
2. If you were this voter list the factors in order of importance as they would affect your decision.
3. Illustrate each of the factors you have identified with other sample quotations as examples.

A simulation

These are to be the three candidates in your federal riding who will contest an upcoming federal election.

Mr. A is a 36-year-old electrician whose name became better known when he was elected to be a labour leader and helped to negotiate an end to a serious strike. Mr. A is a dynamic speaker, but he feels most at home among blue-collar workers. He, his wife, and their four children have been life-long residents of the community. Mr. A has been very active in work among young people in the area.

Mrs. B. is a 45-year-old widow, the mother of a teenaged son and daughter. Her deceased husband was the incumbent Member of Parliament for the riding. Mrs. B has served two terms on the Board of Education and been a busy volunteer with her church projects and with several local charities.

Mr. C is a 30-year-old lawyer whose law firm is very prosperous. His grandfather was an immigrant from an Eastern European country, and his father served several terms on the municipal council. Mr. C is a university graduate, a "sharp" dresser and a quick-thinker. He is married and the father of two children.

Choose one of these candidates and
1. associate this person with a national party;
2. list what you feel would be the issues, both local and national, in this election if it were held six weeks from now;
3. state your candidate's ideas on these issues;
4. act as the campaign manager and prepare the strategy, materials and schedules your candidate will use to win this election during the next six weeks;
5. prepare a realistic budget for your plans in 4 based on accurate prices for radio and newspaper advertisements, hall rentals, printing, etc.

8/Party leadership: The internal power struggle

The most important single person in a political party is its leader, for it is the leader who, more than anyone else, determines party policy and strategy and represents the party to the public. Moreover, it is the leader who becomes Prime Minister if his party wins a majority of the seats in the House of Commons. Choosing a leader is therefore a very important event, not only for the candidates who seek the job and the power it may bring, but also for the party, whose chances of success in the next election may depend greatly on the abilities of the person who is chosen.

Whenever the larger parties call delegates from each of their local branches together, it usually is for important discussions. This type of meeting is called a convention.

The most common type of convention is the policy convention, when party members assemble to debate the programmes and ideas their party is presenting to the nation.

The most interesting type of convention is a leadership convention. Here party members from across the country decide what man or woman they want to lead their national party organization.

A leadership convention may be necessary for a number of reasons. The present leader may be retiring and the convention will have to pick his successor. The one who has led the party may have died, and for a time the party has had no authorized leader. Perhaps some party members want to challenge the old leader, even if he does not want to step down.

Senior party members will have been watching this process carefully. Those who are famous throughout the country, those who are well-liked within the party and those who simply want to be the new leader will all have weighed their chances. Some announce their candidacy; others may throw their support behind another candidate.

Each person who wants to be the party leader will develop an organization to run his own campaign within the party. Once the name of a delegate is submitted to the chairman of the convention these candidates and their workers will try to meet with him. They want delegates' votes and their support.

At the convention the various candidates hold conferences, dances, parties, dinners, briefings, any activity at all, to communicate with the delegates. The results of their efforts are known when each delegate secretly casts his ballot for the person he thinks will do the best job.

Case study: the 1968 Liberal convention

All the partying, the balloons, the fancy hats, the pretty girls, the signs, the bands, the badges and the literature may help to create a livelier atmosphere in the convention hall. But when a delegate enters the voting booth he should try to assess which of the candidates will do the best job for the country.

In 1967 Lester Pearson announced his intention to retire as leader of the Liberal Party and thereby give up the position of Prime Minister. He would not support any particular Liberal who wanted his job, he said, because he wanted the members of his party to make fair choices without considering his own personal preferences.

In April 1968 Liberal delegates from across Canada came to Ottawa to select Mr. Pearson's successor.

The main contenders for the leadership were almost all members of Mr. Pearson's Cabinet.

Joe Greene	— Minister of Agriculture
Paul Hellyer	— Minister of Transport
Eric Kierans	— A Montreal economist
Paul Martin	— Secretary of State for External Affairs
Allan MacEachen	— Minister of Health and Welfare
Pierre E. Trudeau	— Minister of Justice
John Turner	— Registrar-General
Robert Winters	— Minister of Trade

To win the convention, a candidate needed a simple majority from the 2,396 delegates.

This case study sums up the struggle for victory among the eight serious candidates.

WEDNESDAY — PRE-CONVENTION: THE ARRIVALS

Everything was tumult on the platform of Union Station from the moment Trudeau's train arrived at 2:20 p.m. He had ridden up from Montreal aboard a coach chartered for him and his party. He was mobbed by reporters, cameramen and wildly enthusiastic supporters, including several of the growing number of cabinet ministers now behind him and a great many young people, some carrying home-made signs. Cameramen crushed around as he walked down through the tunnel from the platform into the station.

THURSDAY — CONVENTION DAY ONE: THE MEETINGS

On the opening morning of the convention, Thursday, April 4, Trudeau attended a delegates' breakfast at the Skyline Hotel, had a haircut, then arrived at the convention arena in Lansdowne Park at 10 o'clock — the only candidate to arrive at the scheduled time for the official opening. The main item was a speech of welcome by Prime Minister Pearson, and Trudeau wanted to show his respect for the retiring leader by being on time. The vast arena was almost deserted as he and his party arrived, however and he spent a quarter of an hour in his trailer behind the building. Then he entered by a main door and made his way down to the floor of the arena, using his passage to greet and talk briefly with the slowly multiplying smatterings of delegates collecting for the convention opening — which was nearly an hour late.

Taking his place in his box in the arena, Trudeau was flanked by six cabinet ministers and surrounded by a fleet of newsmen. In the adjoining box with his wife sat John Turner. A little way to Trudeau's right sat Paul Martin and his aging supporters . . . His restless movements during the morning brought Martin briefly to Trudeau's box. "We're in for an interesting battle," he said after greeting Trudeau in French.

During the three afternoon workshops there was further confirmation of the Trudeau groundswell. Twenty-five minutes were allotted to each candidate for a prepared speech or a speech and question period. Trudeau kept to his successful campaign technique of a short opening statement, then questions and answers.

By the end of the workshop sessions on Thursday afternoon, the other candidates were deeply concerned by the unmistakeable evidence that Trudeau was not merely drawing the largest crowds and the most attention, but was virtually dominating the entire convention. With each performance, his statements were clearer, sharper, his speaking style better suited to the large crowds listening.

Thursday night, the 8,000 delegates, alternates and visitors in the Lansdowne Park arena bid an official farewell to the retiring Prime Minister, Lester Pearson.

FRIDAY — CONVENTION DAY TWO: THE SPEECHES

On Friday night the really serious business of the convention began. Televised live across Canada on both networks, the candidates would make their final open bid for delegate support.

The ground rules were, of course, the same for all candidates. They had a total of thirty minutes and could use it as they wished, but they were expected to have their main demonstrations at the beginning, and then be certain to have their people out of the way when it was time for the next candidate.

The full complement of the Governor-General's Foot Guards band took part in the well-organized demonstration for Paul Martin when the time came for him to lead off the crucial nomination speeches. Paul Hellyer marched like an embarrassed marionette at the head of his demonstration, so strained that he did not notice when the music stopped and went on doing his stiff little goose step without accompaniment. Agriculture Minister Joe Greene single-handedly stole the show from them all, up to that point, with a standup political speech that won him the first standing ovation of the night without benefit of band and demonstrators — and more votes on the first ballot than even he had expected.

Then Senator Nichol invited Trudeau to take the stand.

Trudeau's strategy was different: no band and no single organized group of demonstrators — just plenty of burnt-orange Trudeau banners and posters distributed strategically throughout the arena, to be put into every willing hand available.

Convention hoopla — Paul Hellyer and his cheerleaders

VISION+
DECISION
=HELLYER
PAUL
HELLYER
WELCOMES
BRITISH COLUMBIA
Youth +
Experience=
Y
E
R

It was also part of the strategy to have known Trudeau supporters in groups of fifteen to twenty placed in this same pattern to add to the impression that the whole arena was breaking out for Trudeau.

... When Trudeau came to the end of his speech, Hellyer — who had stood and applauded Joe Greene — sat silent and smoldering with angry disappointment. Only the supporters around Martin, Hellyer, Kierans and Winters were not all on their feet. It was not a happy moment for any of them and their faces showed it.

SATURDAY — CONVENTION DAY THREE: THE VOTING

For Trudeau, the last day of the Convention began with a pancake and maple-syrup breakfast at the Chateau Laurier ballroom, where some six hundred delegates turned up before it ended.

As he had done at similar breakfasts earlier in the week, he wandered from table to table, meeting and talking to the delegates, always very informal and comfortable. His charm never failed ... As he offered a little wave of goodbye at the end of his Saturday breakfast visit, his guests spontaneously rose at their tables, some of them still munching pancakes, to send him on his way with a standing ovation ...

Senator Nichol, the convention chairman, welcomed the delegates, and explained the voting rules. Balloting was scheduled to begin at 1:00 p.m., but like every schedule at every convention, this was optimistic. There was almost an hour's delay before the voting began, and it was not until about 2:30 that Nichol rose on the stand to announce the results of the first ballot:

Results of first ballot

Greene	169
Hellyer	330
Kierans	103
MacEachen	165
Martin	277
Trudeau	752
Turner	277
Winters	293

The results came as a surprise to nearly every candidate. Trudeau was the principal exception. Enjoying a comfortable lead, he had received approximately the figure his computer had anticipated.

Drops of perspiration appeared on Hellyer's face as he sat popping lifesavers into his mouth after the result was announced by Senator Nichol.

Even before the results were announced, Martin had started scribbling a withdrawal statement on the back of one of the vote scorecards that had been a part of his convention promotion literature. One sentence he did not use in the final version that was turned in to Nichol was: "I have been caught in a generation gap." "Over the years," he told newsmen, "I have learned how important it is to be gracious in victory, and generous and serene in defeat. That is my mood and my composure now." He never lost his dignity; he withdrew from his lifelong ambition with, as Pearson later put it, "gallantry and chivalry." To tearful supporters commiserating with him, he cheerfully teased: "Why don't you all smile? The country is still going to go on. The party is going to go on, and I am going to go on — stronger than ever."

Results of second ballot

Greene	104
Hellyer	465
MacEachen	11
Trudeau	964
Turner	347
Winters	473

Winters now approached Hellyer about dropping out in his favour. "Is there anything we should do?" he asked. But if the rumors that had reached the Trudeau camp that morning about a gang-up deal among the Martin-Winters-Hellyer organizations had ever had real substance, they now proved to have been an unnecessary worry. Hellyer at first said: "I don't know." He then conferred with Judy LaMarsh, who with other backers urged him to pull out in support of Winters.

Hellyer refused their advice. Instead he jumped to his feet and led his supporters in a new round of cheers for himself.

Results of third ballot

Greene	29
Hellyer	377
Trudeau	1051
Turner	279
Winters	621

Within seconds of the third ballot announcement, Hellyer stood up, waved his arm in a cheerleader's gesture and shouted: "Go, Bob, go!" Then he waded across to Winters' nearby box and raised the Trade Minister's hand, struggling courageously to hide his profound disappointment. It had not turned out like his slick organization and its sophisticated computer had said at all. Joe Greene, all the sentiment gone from his backing, was dropped off the ballot as the low man on the last vote, with just 29. He headed straight for Trudeau's box.

That left in John Turner, who had fallen back to 279, but now held a possibly crucial influence on the next ballot had he been prepared to play power-broker for keeps. But Turner had been saying all along: "No deals." After the second ballot, Trudeau backer Harold (Sunny) Gordon, a young Montreal lawyer who had once been Executive Assistant to Sauvé and had been an early member of the Montreal group who finally emerged as the

key strategists in the Trudeau campaign, had tried to sway Turner to quit in favour of the Justice Minister. He made an approach to Turner aide Gerry Grafstein. But Grafstein was not buying: "You can't promise him anything but a cabinet job, and he's got to be included anyway."

Finally the fourth ballot began. By now it was early evening. The terrific tension and strain of the proceedings had taken a toll on all the candidates including Trudeau.

Then Senator Nichol read the results of the fourth ballot: Trudeau — 1,203 .... An enormous roar almost drowned out the other results; Turner — 195; Winters — 954. The Liberal party had a new leader, the country a new Prime Minister.

From *Journey to Power* by Donald Peacock

QUESTIONS

1. What factors did delegates at this leadership convention consider in selecting the candidates for which they voted?
2. What aspects of a convention could detract from the delegates' ability to make careful decisions?
3. It has been suggested that Mr. Trudeau won the convention because he brought a fresh approach to convention campaigning. What evidence seems to support this theory?
4. To what extent may a person's political career be determined by decisions made before and during a leadership convention? To answer this completely, you should find out what happened to the political careers of the unsuccessful candidates.
5. What kind of personal favours might the winning candidate be expected to honour following the convention? How can he repay these favours?

Pierre Trudeau addresses the delegates

The winner

Case study: the 1976 Conservative convention

In February 1976 the Progressive Conservatives held a national convention in Ottawa to elect a new leader for their party. Later that year they released the figures to show the costs to organize the convention and also the revenue and expenses for the individual candidates.

These figures show just how expensive politics at this high level can be. It cost the Conservative Party over $600,000 to run the convention, and of this amount more than $260,000 was required just to pay for the building and other physical facilities needed for staging the convention.

In this section we shall examine the financial data to see how the candidates raised their money and how they spent it. We shall then consider some of the important issues which these figures raise.

Joe Clark celebrates his election as leader of the Progressive Conservative Party. Mr. Clark (at 36 the youngest leader in the party's history) won a surprise victory on the fourth ballot, narrowly defeating Claude Wagner.

As a condition of becoming a candidate, the party asked each nominee to submit a report on the finances to run his campaign.

The report of Brian Mulroney, a Montreal lawyer, was eagerly anticipated because it was believed that his campaign was the most lavishly funded and executed; some journalists even speculated that his costs were near $350,000. Mr. Mulroney refused to reveal his report, however, because he objected to its being made public. In a letter to the party president, he said that he had promised his donors that their names would be revealed to the party executive but never to the public and that the party's later decision to make all the reports public would force him to violate his word. Rather than breach this trust, he would not reveal his financial situation.

The following chart summarizes the expenses and revenue for seven of the candidates.

REVENUE

Total of contributions under $25	Total of contributions $25-$100	Money or value received in sums of more than $1000	Total contributions	Candidate
0	129,034.81	28,862.50	**157,897.31**	**Joe Clark** MP, Rocky Mountain. Winner on fourth ballot.
109.78	34,332.55	6,000.00	**40,442.33**	**Heward Grafftey** MP, Brome-Missisquoi. Went to Clark team after first ballot, in which he got lowest vote total.
340.00	32,930.00	48,687.00	**81,957.00**	**Paul Hellyer** Newspaper columnist, businessman, and former Liberal Cabinet Minister. Went to Wagner after first ballot.
122,819.19		3,500.00	**126,319.19**	**Flora MacDonald** MP, Kingston and the Islands. Went to Clark team after second ballot.
0	4,541.25	0	**4,541.25**	**R.C. Quittenton** Windsor community college president. Dropped out before first ballot.
2,244.00	62,605.89	49,214.96	**114,064.85**	**Sinclair Stevens** MP, York Simcoe. Went to Clark team after first ballot.
800.00	108,345.00	54,715.00	**163,860.00**	**Claude Wagner** MP, St. Hyacinthe. Lost to Clark on fourth ballot.

1.   Write down your impressions, observations and questions about these reports. Be prepared to discuss these as a class.

2.   One of these candidates had little trouble raising money toward paying his deficit; in fact he received donations of almost $90,000 in three months after the convention. Which one would this be? How can you account for this?

3.   It is always obvious that there can only be one winner. What reasons might prompt candidates to run for this position even when it is generally accepted that chances are greater that they will lose rather than win?

4.   The PC Party announced after the reports were submitted that it would consider rebating each candidate 50% of the outstanding balance or $30,000, whichever was less. This rebate would still leave some candidates with major debts.

EXPENDITURES

Total expenditures	Travel	Advertising and printing	Accommodation	Staff assistance	Communications	Other
168,353.69	13,098.15	39,931.00	16,567.07	7,917.90	15,747.88	75,091.69
83,845.92	23,947.77	16,652.24	4,533.34	17,601.81	2,321.47	18,789.29
287,786.00	22,476.00	128,339.00	66,540.00	18,233.00	30,946.00	21,252.00
152,704.01	16,647.19	63,333.01	17,310.89	22,717.81	10,344.91	22,350.20
9,335.82	877.05	5,130.00	1,869.36	177.72	392.82	888.87
294,106.58	41,282.50	144,741.03	35,683.08	45,962.38	7,403.31	19,034.28
266,538.21	34,676.76	74,917.40	36,443.68	83,887.00	24,805.15	11,808.22

Do you consider it fair that a person willing to lead his party and the country be left with such debts? Should a party try to limit candidates' expenses? How might it do this?

5. In Britain, the party caucus, rather than a national convention, chooses the leader. What would be the advantages and the disadvantages of this method? Would this be a better method for Canadian political parties to use?

6. The following three reports indicate in a greater depth the nature of their candidates' fund-raising. Try to find the unique characteristics of each report.

Candidate: Claude Wagner

Name	Nature of Contribution	Amount or Value
Inland Publishing	Cash	$ 5,000
Conrad Black	Cash	$15,000
Lake Ontario Cement	Cash	$ 5,000
Draper Dobie	Cash	$12,000
Roman Corp.	Cash	$ 5,000

Candidate: Paul Hellyer

Name	Nature of Contribution	Amount or Value
*Denison Mines Limited	Cheque	$10,000
Lake Ontario Cement Ltd.	Cheque	$ 5,000
Race-Hellyer Ginseng Growers Ltd.	Cheque	$ 2,000
*Roman Corporation Limited	Cheque	$ 5,000
Paul T. Hellyer	Cheque	$25,000
Trinity Progressive Conservative Association	Cheque	$ 1,687

*owned by same man, Mr. S. Roman

Candidate: Pat Nowlan

Name	Nature of Contribution	Amount or Value
Rolland Thornhill	Cash	$ 1,950
Pat Nowlan, M.P.	Cash	$ 5,000
Linda Logan	Services	$ 2,000
Diane Foran	Services	$ 1,400
Anne Corrigan	Services	$ 1,100
Clara Jefferson	Services	$ 1,500
Mike Kontac	Services	$ 1,500
Anne Harris	Services	$ 1,200
Hanson Dowell	Services	$ 5,000

9/Bienvenue à Ottawa— welcome to Ottawa

"Good day, ladies and gentlemen, and welcome aboard our guided tour of the city of Ottawa, Canada's national capital. It will be my pleasure to escort this bus and to offer some commentary as we pass by the highlights of the city. Your driver and I encourage you to relax and enjoy our time together.

"While we are making our way to the first location on the tour perhaps I could tell you something of the history of this city. The original settlement here was founded by Colonel John By, a British army engineer who was given orders to build a canal on the Rideau River. Bytown, as the village was called, became a convenient stop for vessels using the canal to bypass the St. Lawrence rapids on their journeys between Montreal and Kingston.

"In 1858 it was Queen Victoria who chose the site to be the seat of government for the colony of Canada. At that time Canada was the name of just one of several British North American colonies. Its territory included regions of the present provinces of Ontario and Quebec.

"Each of these regions felt that it should be the seat of the colony's administration, at least for a few months of the year. When the representatives and government workers became tired of journeying back and forth between Canada East and Canada West, the government decided to ask Queen Victoria to suggest a permanent site for the capital.

"Four cities — Quebec, Montreal, Kingston and Toronto — sought the nomination, but the Queen's selection was Ottawa.

"Some historians have said that she made this choice because Ottawa was on the border between Canada East and Canada West. Its location made it a compromise spot.

"Other people have suggested that the Duke of Wellington, the great hero of the Battle of Waterloo, advised Her Majesty of the strategic value of Ottawa's site. The town could easily be reached by water because it was on the junction of rivers whose system joined with the St. Lawrence

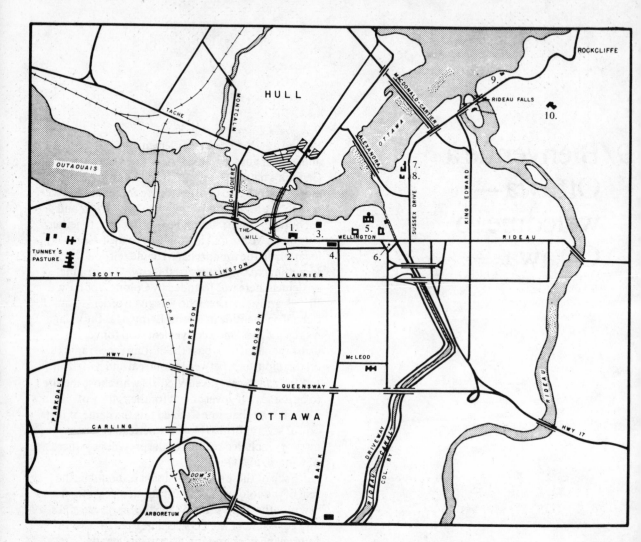

Ottawa — a map of the tour

1. National Library
2. Garden of the Provinces
3. Supreme Court
4. Bank of Canada
5. Parliament Hill
6. Confederation Square
7. The Mint
8. War Museum
9. 24 Sussex Dr.
10. Rideau Hall

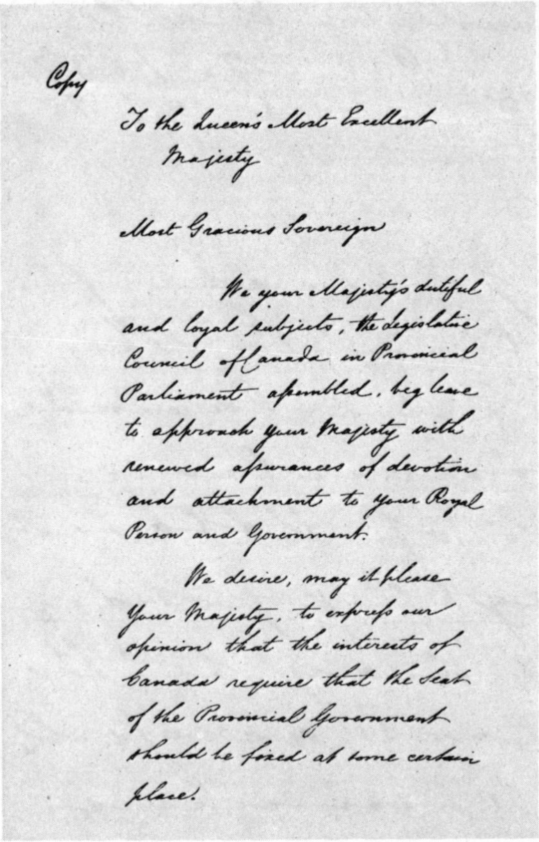

To the Queen's Most Excellent
Majesty

Most Gracious Sovereign

We your Majesty's dutiful
and loyal subjects, the Legislative
Council of Canada in Provincial
Parliament assembled, beg leave
to approach your Majesty with
renewed assurances of devotion
and attachment to your Royal
Person and Government.

We desire, may it please
Your Majesty, to express our
opinion that the interests of
Canada require that the Seat
of the Provincial Government
should be fixed at some certain
place.

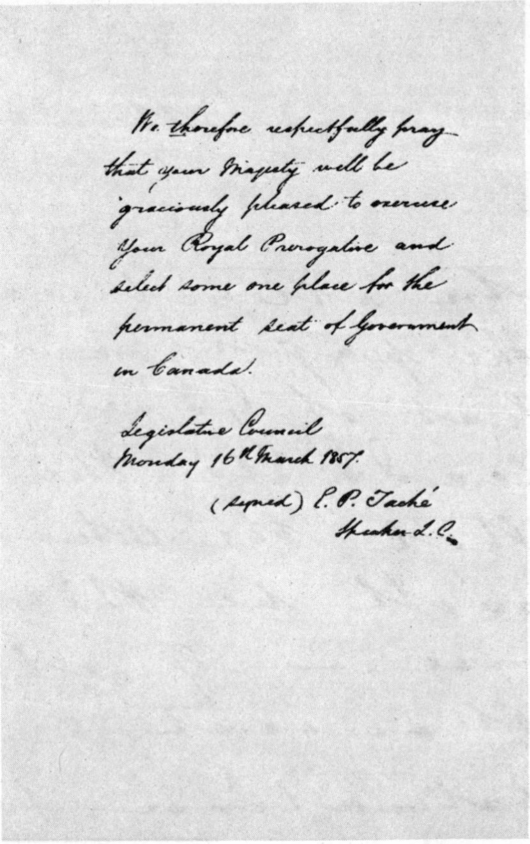

We therefore respectfully pray
that your Majesty will be
graciously pleased to exercise
Your Royal Prerogative and
select some one place for the
permanent Seat of Government
in Canada.

Legislative Council
Monday 16th March 1857.

(signed) E. P. Taché
Speaker L. C.

On March 16, 1857 the Province of Canada sent this letter to Queen Victoria, asking her to decide which city should be their capital.

Windsor Castle.
Oct: 27. 1857.

Memodm

An attentive perusal of
the papers relative to the
Seat of Governmt in Canada
leads to the conviction
that the choice of Ottawa
will be the right & politic
one. — Quebec may be the
strongest & most accessible
situation for communi

St Lawrence — say at Prescot
or Brockville or Cornwall
which an American force
crossing the St Lawrence to
attack the new capital
could not with safety leave
in their rear. —

Portions of a royal memorandum recommending that Ottawa be chosen as Canada's capital. The handwriting on this copy is Prince Albert's and the initials at the bottom are Queen Victoria's.

and eventually the ocean. Yet it was not located at a spot too close to the United States. If troubles ever erupted between the colony and its southern neighbour, Ottawa would not be in immediate danger of capture.

"In 1867 when the three colonies of New Brunswick, Nova Scotia and Canada became a nation, the Fathers of Confederation adopted the name of the one colony as the name of their new country and its capital city became the capital of the nation too.

"We have now come to the beginning of the tour. We are driving slowly along Wellington Street, parallel to the Ottawa River. On your left is one of the newest government buildings in the city. This is the National Library of Canada where copies of every book published in our country are deposited. With eighty miles of shelves it certainly has space for many books.

"Another part of this building houses the Public Archives of Canada, the official records of our history. Thousands of books, maps, pictures, letters and official documents are preserved here in special fireproof and humidity-controlled rooms. Some of the items are hundreds of years old; others are only as old as yesterday.

"To your right now is the Garden of the Provinces, four acres of parkland opened in 1962 by Prime Minister John Diefenbaker. Each of the provincial and territorial crests, flowers and flags is displayed here.

"Beside the Garden are two massive structures, the Veterans' Affairs Building and the Trade and Commerce Building. These are the first of many government departments which have their national headquarters either here in Ottawa or across the river in the city of Hull, Quebec.

"Large buildings like these were originally put near the centre of the city, but today government departments are turning away from this area in favour of planned developments such as Tunney's Pasture where the Department of National Health and Welfare, The National Film Board, and Atomic Energy of Canada have their headquarters on the outskirts of the city. You can imagine the difference these moves have made for our traffic problems in downtown Ottawa!

"On your left we are approaching the Supreme Court Building, home of Canada's highest court. Near it, but looking rather older, are the Justice and Finance Department Buildings.

"At the present time, ladies and gentlemen, you are driving over a fortune because the Bank of Canada, whose headquarters are appearing on your right, keeps much of our national gold and currency in two levels of heavy vaults under Wellington Street. Other large insurance companies and banks also have their offices close to the centre of Ottawa, just like our national bank here.

"We have arrived now at Parliament Hill, the first stop of the tour. This area, with its three distinct buildings set on a bluff overlooking the Ottawa River, is one of the most photographed sights in Canada.

"Each of the structures on Parliament Hill is called a Block. The Centre Block, with the Peace Tower in front, is the main building. In this Block are the two rooms or chambers where the men and women who make our laws meet to decide on national affairs.

"The House of Commons is located in the left or western part of the building as you enter the main doors. The Senate Chamber is to your right. Straight ahead through Confederation Hall, as the main entrance is called, is a corridor leading to the Parliamentary Library.

"Scattered throughout the Centre Block are offices for some MPs, the Prime Minister, and other government officials. There are also several rooms where committees and delegations can meet.

"The building also contains the working rooms for the national press and for other government employees such as the guards who patrol the

The Garden of the Provinces

The Supreme Court

The Parliament Buildings — the Centre Block and the Peace Tower

buildings and the assistants who work with the MP s.

"This is actually the second Centre Block. The original structure was destroyed by fire in 1916. Only the Library, which was at the rear, was saved. In the grounds behind the Block and the Library you can still see a large bell which hung in the first tower. It is mounted as a memorial to victims of the 1916 disaster.

"The Parliamentary Library had its own fire in 1952. However, every effort was made to restore its original beauty. With its wooden carvings, statue of Queen Victoria and tiers of books along the walls, this library is a grand place for the MPs and Senators to do research for their projects in Parliament.

"The present Centre Block, one storey larger than the original, was finished in 1922. A larger tower, called the Peace Tower to remind people of the world war in which Canada had fought a decade earlier, was completed in 1927. By a law of the city of Ottawa, no building is to be higher than this tower; the highest point of the Parliament Buildings must always stand out against the city's skyline.

"The Peace Tower contains a Memorial Chamber dedicated to the Canadian citizens who died during all the wars in which we have participated. The names of these persons are inscribed in special books in the Chamber. Every day one page of each book is turned with great solemnity. In this way the name of every one of Canada's war dead is honoured publicly once each year.

"The Peace Tower also holds a carillon. This is a musical instrument with 53 bells that weigh from ten pounds to over eleven tons. You can hear it played during periods of national celebrations and at regular concerts throughout the year.

"At the summit of the Tower, just below the large Canadian flag, is an observation deck. From here you have a magnificent view not only of the city of Ottawa but also the city of Hull.

"The East and West Blocks, which were constructed with the original Centre Block over a century ago, have not changed in their gothic style of architecture. Today the East Block contains the Prime Minister's main office and also the Cabinet Room where he meets with his advisers. The West Block holds more offices for MPs; this building is connected by a tunnel to the Centre Block.

"Before we leave Parliament Hill, you might like to wander around the grounds, which are always open to visitors. The bus will park here for one hour to give you time to explore the buildings and the grounds.

"Scattered around the hill are the statues of famous figures from our history. Some of the statues, such as the figure of Queen Victoria beside the West Block and the memorial to George-Étienne Cartier, are the work of Louis Philippe Hébert, Canada's most famous sculptor of the nineteenth century.

"The lawns in front of the buildings are used in the summer for the colourful ceremony of the Changing of the Guard by a regiment of scarlet-tuniced soldiers.

"On the walkway that leads from Wellington Street to the Centre Block be sure to see the Centennial Flame and Fountain. The Flame was lit by Prime Minister Pearson at midnight, New Year's Eve, 1966, to begin the centennial celebrations of 1967. The Fountain features the crests of our provinces and territories, the same designs which you can see carved into the stone of the arch at the base of the Peace Tower.

"From Parliament Hill, ladies and gentlemen, we turn left and enter Confederation Square. In the centre of the Square stands our nation's main monument to the soldiers of our wars. This structure was officially unveiled in 1939 by King George VI, the father of Queen Elizabeth, while he was in Ottawa on a national tour. Just a few months after he dedicated this spot to the memory of the Candians who had died in World War I, the world

The old Centre Block

The fire of 1916

Parliament Hill about 1920. The new Centre Block, without the Peace Tower, is almost finished.

Changing the Guard

was at war again. Each year, on November 11, and throughout the year when an important visitor from another country wants to honour Canada's war efforts, the official ceremonies are conducted right at this monument.

"Just beyond the War Memorial on your right is Elgin Street where the National Gallery of Canada is located. Five cents in taxes from each Canadian citizen go annually toward the costs of this gallery. Today it houses a valuable collection with thousands of paintings, prints, drawings and sculptures. May I suggest that you visit the Gallery to enjoy some of these items that you have already helped to buy for the country.

"We turn left beside the Chateau Laurier and enter Sussex Drive, one of the most famous streets in the capital. Notice the city market on your right and the old shops which are being preserved in the style of 1867. Here, on the left, are long wooden structures which look like military barracks but which are actually temporary buildings constructed during World War II but still in use today.

"On the left now is the Canadian War Museum with its collection of military hardware going back to the regiments in the colony of New France. One of its most prized displays is the uniform worn by General Brock during the Battle of Queenston Heights in the War of 1812-14. On the jacket you can still see the bullet hole from the fatal shot which Brock received.

"Beside this museum is The Royal Canadian Mint. Here old coins are melted down and new coins manufactured. Medals are struck here for the armed forces, and special commemorative plaques and medals are produced for the government's use. The Mint also refines gold bullion for the government and private mines.

"Guarding the Mint is the complete responsibility of the Royal Canadian Mounted Police. You might say that on Parliament Hill a visitor can see the changing of the guard, while here you see the guarding of the change.

"Now we can see the modern Macdonald-Cartier Bridge which joins Hull and Ottawa, and beyond it, also on the left, a National Research Council laboratory where many important Canadian inventions are developed. It was here, for example, that scientists made important progress towards improving radar during World War II.

"Sussex Drive crosses the Rideau River now as we drive across Green Island. The Ottawa City Hall is to your right. From the other side of the bus you can see a falls where the Rideau River pours into the Ottawa. Hidden behind this curtain of water is a secret ledge from which the Indians ambushed intruders.

"Again on your right you can see the huge brown building that looks like an ancient fortified citadel. This is the new headquarters for Canada's Department of External Affairs, where all of our official business with other countries is controlled.

"Now we are beginning to enter a quieter part of the city. On the left, for example, is Earnscliffe, the home of the British High Commissioner, the British government's representative in Canada. For a time this was the residence of Canada's first Prime Minister; here in 1891 Sir John died.

"Beside Earnscliffe is the Embassy of France, the official headquarters for the government of France and their highest representative, their ambassador, in Canada. From here it is the ambassador's job to report what is happening in Canada to his home government.

"This embassy is only one of scores of embassies in Ottawa. Each nation which Canada officially recognizes is entitled to have such a building and to post their representatives, called diplomats, to our capital, just as we post diplomats to their capital cities. As we drive by these embassies we may not realize how busy they are and how necessary their role is in our national affairs. Each ambassador throughout the city uses his staff to watch what is happening in Canadian affairs and decide how this will affect his own nation. A country with fishing

The Royal Canadian Mint

interests around the world, for example, would expect their ambassador to inform them if Canada placed new restrictions on the use of waters along our coasts where their fishermen make catches.

"An ambassador such as the French ambassador is expected to represent his country at official ceremonies such as the opening of Parliament. He may also travel throughout Canada making speeches or attending functions which concern his nation.

"Throughout the year, and especially on days important to his own country's history, the ambassador may host parties for other nations' representatives as well as Canadian guests in his embassy.

"If a Canadian citizen needs information about France he could write to the staff of this building and receive a reply to his request. If business people want to locate contacts for their businesses in France, an embassy officer could assist them. If students need information about France for a project at school, a member of the embassy staff could help them too.

"All these duties keep each embassy's personnel very busy. Some countries add even more responsibilities because they use their staffs to issue a travel permit called a visa to each foreign citizen who hopes to visit them.

"If the embassy represents a nation that is very large or very active in its dealings with Canadians then it may also be responsible for offices, called consulates, in other Canadian cities where the local citizens can deal directly with a government representative. Montreal, Toronto and Vancouver are generally the cities where foreign consulates are established in Canada.

"All the business from embassies as well as our own national business keeps the resident of the next estate on your left very busy. This is 24 Sussex Drive, the home of the Prime Minister of Canada. Only the gateways are visible from the street; large trees hide the house from our view and provide some privacy for the Prime Minister and his family.

If you would like a better view of the residence you must see it from a spot further along the shore or from a ship which sails along the Ottawa River.

"The mansion was built in 1868 by a lumberman Member of Parliament and acquired by our government in 1902 for $140,000. For many years we rented it to the Australian government, but Canada decided to make it the Prime Minister's official residence in 1950.

"The building has three stories with personal family rooms as well as a formal dining room, a library, hall, and a drawing room which together are large enough to hold a reception for two hundred people. It is set on four acres of land atop a bluff at a beautiful spot on the Ottawa River. When the Prime Minister is not in residence here he is generally living at his official summer home in the Gatineau Hills of Quebec.

"On the other side of Sussex Drive is the entrance to the home of the Governor General or the Queen if she should be in Canada. This building is known by two names, Rideau Hall and Government House, and it, too, is hidden from the main roads by many acres of grounds. When the Governor General is in residence it is sometimes possible to see his personal standard flying over the building and the trees around it. When he is not here the grounds are open to the public for their pleasure.

"Government House is used for many official events. It has a large ballroom with throne chairs, an unusual party room decorated like a circus tent, and several comfortable reception areas. Its main entrance is designed to reflect our royal traditions with large paintings of kings and queens. Behind all these public rooms are the private family rooms of the Governor General with the gardens and recreational facilities that can also be used for public functions.

"Beside Rideau Hall's main entrance is another residence, Seven Rideau Gate, the official Canadian guest house into which we welcome distinguished visitors who are staying in our capital.

24 Sussex Drive

PRIME MINISTER'S OFFICIAL RESIDENCE

Question No. 1,666—Mr. Cossitt:

1. What was the total cost for all aspects of the Prime Minister's Official residence in Ottawa for the fiscal year 1973-74 including a breakdown of the total showing (a) insofar as the National Capital Commission is concerned (b) insofar as the Department of Public Works is concerned (c) insofar as the Prime Minister's and the Privy Council Offices are concerned?

2. For each, what is the breakdown of costs under all possible headings including (a) salaries and wages (b) contract services (c) supplies (d) sundries and entertainment (e) construction and alterations (f) maintenance?

Hon. Mitchell Sharp (President of the Privy Council): I am informed by the National Capital Commission, the Department of Public Works and the Prime Minister's and Privy Council Offices as follows: 1.

		(a)	(b)	(c)
	(a)	$36,927.00	$221,005.03	$73,053.00
2.	(a)	$21,566.00	$ 4,438.27	$54,694.00
	(b)	1,809.00	126,570.17	Nil
	(c)	4,646.00	89,196.53	12,739.00
	(d)	559.00	800.06	5,620.00
	(e)	8,347.00	800.06	Nil
	(f)	Broken down under (a) to (d)	800.06	Nil

PRIME MINISTER'S OFFICIAL RESIDENCE

Question No. 1,667—Mr. Cossitt:

1. What was the total cost for all aspects of the Prime Minister's Official residence in Ottawa for the fiscal year 1974-75 up to and including the last month for which figures are available, including a breakdown of the total showing (a) insofar as the National Capital Commission is concerned (b) insofar as the Department of Public Works is concerned (c) insofar as the Prime Minister's and the Privy Council Offices are concerned?

2. For each, what is the breakdown of costs under all possible headings including (a) salaries and wages (b) contract services (c) supplies (d) sundries and entertainment (e) construction and alterations (f) maintenance?

Hon. Mitchell Sharp (President of the Privy Council): I am informed by the National Capital Commission, the Department of Public Works and the Prime Minister's and Privy Council Offices as follows: 1.

Order Paper Questions

		(a)	(b)	(c)
	(a)	$31,322.00	$46,048.00	$77,405.00
2.	(a)	$20,347.00	$ 3,712.00	$61,405.00
	(b)	2,155.00	37,138.00	Nil
	(c)	5,896.00	3,577.00	15,000.00
	(d)	108.00	1,621.00	1,000.00
	(e)	2,816.00	1,621.00	Nil
	(f)	Broken down under (a) to (d)	1,621.00	Nil

The Prime Minister's residence — Questions in Parliament

Rideau Hall

During our centennial year when so many foreign leaders came to Canada, this house was their residence while they were in Ottawa.

"The last part of our tour will be a quiet drive by the village of Rockcliffe, a small community within the boundaries of the city of Ottawa. Rockcliffe is a residential area where many of the ambassadors, senior government officials, and prosperous local residents make their homes. One of the houses here is Stornoway House where the Leader of the Opposition lives. Like 24 Sussex Drive this is a residence owned by the Canadian nation and maintained by our Department of Public Works. Stornoway House, however, is much smaller than the Prime Minister's home.

"As we return along Sussex Drive to the centre of the city we ought to note the work of the National Capital Commission, for it is this group which supervises all the plans and developments of the area to make Ottawa a beautiful city. Twenty citizens from across the country make up the Commission, but eight hundred employees carry out the blueprints of development.

"The Commission was established by Parliament in 1959, but its work has been guided by the ideas of a French town planner, Jacques Greber, whom Prime Minister Mackenzie King invited to develop a master plan for Ottawa. More green spaces and parks, the removal of railway lines from the core of the city, the restoration and conservation of historic buildings and an overall plan to control the growth of the region have been part of the Commission's work.

"We hope you have enjoyed your tour of Canada's capital and that you will try to see all the other national buildings and city highlights which are beyond the limits of our tour today."

And what did you think of Ottawa?

A sub-arctic lumber village converted by royal mandate into a political cockpit.

Attributed to Goldwin Smith

A Capital is the *reflection*, the *symbol* of the whole nation. The Capital of Canada, as in all federated states, such as in the case of Washington, or Berne, has *special* importance; it is the city which, to every Canadian and to all foreigners, must be representative of all of the ten confederated provinces, without, however, prejudicing the attributes and prerogatives of their respective capitals.

Chosen for this noble role by a far-seeing and wisely inspired Queen, the little Ontario town of Ottawa, the outgrowth of the pioneer village of Bytown, rapidly became a large city, and, with distances gradually losing their significance, blended itself with the neighbouring villages and localities around the beautiful Ottawa River, formerly a frontier but now a link between the two provinces of Ontario and Quebec, which are symbolic of Canadian greatness . . . .

The planning of the Capital is therefore a *national undertaking, of which each Canadian can be proud* and through which national desires and aspirations can be expressed through material accomplishments.

Jacques Greber

I would not wish to say anything disparaging of the capital, but it is hard to say anything good of it. Ottawa is not a handsome city and does not appear destined to become one either.

Sir Wilfrid Laurier

It's not easy running the littlest embassy in Ottawa

The Embassy of Lebanon sits on a slightly down-at-the-heels street in the south end of Ottawa, a tribute to man's ability to conduct international diplomacy on a budget of practically nothing.

Let other nations present a posh front to the world with their grand official buildings, chauffeured limousines, sumptuous receptions, fleets of vice-consuls and military attachés. Lebanon, an Arab country, runs a very tight ship by comparison. With its utilitarian 20- by 40-foot red brick quarters, Lebanon is the teensiest of Ottawa's 60 embassies and high commissions — with the possible exceptions of a few embassies temporarily quartered in apartments and offices. Certainly, you won't find a smaller staff anywhere — the man to see for everything is the ambassador, Dr. Alif Gebara, who runs the place with a smile, a lot of nerve and three stenographers. No assistants. No counsellors. No cultural affairs secretaries. Just an annual budget of $75,000 to operate an embassy and residence. And the home office in Beirut even tried to cut that this year.

Dr. Gebara (his doctorate is in law) suspects he has the tiniest budget in Ottawa's embassy business. Not that he wishes to complain, understand, but the U.S. Embassy has a staff of 70 in Ottawa. You could put the entire Lebanese Embassy offices in its main waiting room. When a group of 30 Arab students tried to occupy the Lebanese Embassy two years ago to protest Lebanon's attitude to Arab guerrillas, they couldn't all fit in. It's enough to get an ambassador down in the mouth.

The $75,000 may seem like a lot at first glance. But from this His Excellency must pay the day-to-day expenses of embassy and residence, salaries of the three at the embassy and staff of five at the residence, his own salary — about $15,000 — and his travel and entertainment. His Excellency hasn't much left for frivolities. He occasionally has to dip into his own bank account.

Still, with 80,000 Lebanese and Canadians of Lebanese extraction in Canada, Lebanon feels obliged to keep a man in this country. As long as he keeps expenses down.

"For one thing, we don't have any spies," says His Excellency. "Spies are expensive. Only the big countries can afford them. We're too small for that kind of stuff." Dr. Gebara picks up what information he can at receptions and cocktail parties, or meetings with assorted diplomats and government types. Possible changes in government policy, advance info on who's replacing whom in what sensitive job, stuff of that sort. It's not much, but it keeps his superiors in Beirut satisfied.

Once a month, he scribbles what he's learned in longhand, then hands it to his number one man at the embassy to type up in Arabic.

Dr. Gebara also saves money on diplomatic couriers. He has none. For Dr. Gebara's communiques to Beirut, an Air Canada man picks them up in a diplomatic pouch and tosses them aboard the next overseas flight. "They find their way to Beirut eventually," says Dr. Gebara.

He hopes for faster service if he can work out the details of a new air service between Beirut and Montreal, a project he's been working on with the Canadian Government. He expects it'll be ready to begin by the end of this year.

"We could use the tourist business," says Dr. Gebara. When the deal goes through, Dr. Gebara will once again be able to stock his table with Lebanese wines. Despite his pride in his country's rosés, he had to give them up — it was too expensive to transport them without a direct air link to Canada. He had to switch to French wines.

From "It's not easy running the littlest embassy in Ottawa" by Tom Alderman, *The Canadian Magazine,* November 20, 1971

QUESTIONS

1. (a) Using your knowledge of world geography, name four capitals which, like Ottawa, might have been selected because of their strategic location. For each city explain the logic of its location.

(b) Name three other world capitals which were probably chosen for reasons other than their strategic location. The encyclopedias of your school library can help you in the research for this project.

2. There has been some criticism recently that Ottawa is not a suitable site for the capital of Canada. What circumstances might create such criticism? Suggest a reasonable alternate site for a Canadian capital and be sure to give reasons for your selection.

3. The government's views and policies on many national issues will be of interest to the corps of ambassadors in Ottawa. From current events select three items which are of interest now to Canadians. For each one tell how an ambassador would try to influence the government to act so that its policies would suit the interests of his nation.

4. Suppose you were the Canadian ambassador to Venezuela and you decided to host a party there to honour Canada's founding on July 1. Prepare the instructions for decorations, the menu and the entertainment that you feel would make a unique Canadian party for your guests.

5. Find out how other national governments have tried to plan the orderly development of their capitals. Be prepared to show how the principles supported by these other nations could be useful to our National Capital Commission in planning the growth of Ottawa.

6. What future projects could you suggest to the National Capital Commission to make Ottawa an even better city?

Topics for further research

1. Critics of our democratic system suggest that, although we offer the choice of voting for a number of parties, we are really encouraging an expensive, disunifying and repetitive system because our parties are simply too much alike.

(a) To what extent is this a valid criticism?

(b) Research the basic philosophies of our major parties and test these against this criticism.

2. By reviewing Canadian federal election results over the past two decades, assess the validity of the theory that Canada has no truly national political party with strong support in every region.

3. Here is a simplified chart to show the results of a general election. Copy it in your notes and be prepared to answer the questions which follow.

	PARTY A	PARTY B	PARTY C	PARTY D
Constituency #1	5,000 votes	6,000 votes	3,000 votes	4,000 votes
Constituency #2	8,000 votes	3,000 votes	4,000 votes	4,000 votes
Constituency #3	6,000 votes	8,000 votes	5,000 votes	1,000 votes
Constituency #4	6,000 votes	7,000 votes	6,000 votes	1,000 votes

(a) Mark the winning candidate in each constituency.

(b) Circle the party which wins the election and becomes the government.

(c) Total the votes received by each party in all the constituencies.

(d) What weakness within our electoral system becomes evident when you study these results?

(e) Be prepared to discuss this situation with the class. Could you suggest a solution to this weakness?

4. Some countries such as France and West Germany use a different method to distribute seats in their parliaments after the votes are counted. This method is called proportional representation.

(a) Find out what proportional representation is and how it works in France and Germany.

(b) What would be the advantages and disadvantages of proportional representation for Canada?

As part of your research see Chapter 12 of *Divide and Con* by Walter Stewart (New Press, 1973).